Crystallization-Study
of the
**Epistles
of John**

Volume Two

Witness Lee

The Holy Word for Morning Revival

Living Stream Ministry
Anaheim, CA • www.lsm.org

First Edition, August 2007.

ISBN 0-7363-3502-1

Published by

Living Stream Ministry
2431 W. La Palma Ave., Anaheim, CA 92801 U.S.A.
P. O. Box 2121, Anaheim, CA 92814 U.S.A.

Printed in the United States of America

07 08 09 10 11 / 6 5 4 3 2 1

Contents

Preface

1. This book is intended as an aid to believers in developing a daily time of morning revival with the Lord in His word. At the same time, it provides a limited review of the Summer Training held July 2-7, 2007, in Anaheim, California, on the "Crystallization-study of the Epistles of John." Through intimate contact with the Lord in His word, the believers can be constituted with life and truth and thereby equipped to prophesy in the meetings of the church unto the building up of the Body of Christ.

2. The entire content of this book is taken from the *Crystallization-study Outlines: The Epistles of John,* the text and footnotes of the Recovery Version of the Bible, selections from the writings of Witness Lee and Watchman Nee, and *Hymns,* all of which are published by Living Stream Ministry.

3. The book is divided into weeks. One training message is covered per week. Each week presents first the message outline, followed by six daily portions, a hymn, and then some space for writing. The training outline has been divided into days, corresponding to the six daily portions. Each daily portion covers certain points and begins with a section entitled "Morning Nourishment." This section contains selected verses and a short reading that can provide rich spiritual nourishment through intimate fellowship with the Lord. The "Morning Nourishment" is followed by a section entitled "Today's Reading," a longer portion of ministry related to the day's main points. Each day's portion concludes with a short list of references for further reading and some space for the saints to make notes concerning their spiritual inspiration, enlightenment, and enjoyment to serve as a reminder of what they have received of the Lord that day.

4. The space provided at the end of each week is for composing a short prophecy. This prophecy can be composed by considering all of our daily notes, the "harvest" of our inspirations during the week, and preparing a main point

with some sub-points to be spoken in the church meetings for the organic building up of the Body of Christ.

5. Following the last week in this volume, we have provided
reading schedules for both the Old and New Testaments
in the Recovery Version with footnotes. These schedules
are arranged so that one can read through both the Old
and New Testaments of the Recovery Version with footnotes in two years.

6. As a practical aid to the saints' feeding on the Word
throughout the day, we have provided verse cards at the
end of the volume, which correspond to each day's scripture reading. These may be cut out and carried along as a
source of spiritual enlightenment and nourishment in
the saints' daily lives.

7. The *Crystallization-study Outlines* were compiled by
Living Stream Ministry from the writings of Witness
Lee and Watchman Nee. The outlines, footnotes, and
references in the Recovery Version of the Bible are by
Witness Lee. All of the other references cited in this pub-
lication are from the published ministry of Witness Lee
and Watchman Nee.

Summer Training
(July 2-7, 2007)

CRYSTALLIZATION-STUDY
OF
THE EPISTLES OF JOHN

Banners:

The fellowship of the eternal life,
the flow of the eternal life within all the believers,
is the reality of living in the Body of Christ.

We know the Triune God
by experiencing and enjoying Him
as the One who dwells in our spirit and
desires to spread into our heart.

By the anointing of the all-inclusive compound Spirit,
who is the composition of the Divine Trinity,
we know and enjoy the Father, the Son, and
the Spirit as our life and life supply.

The Son of God has given us an understanding
so that we might know the true One,
the genuine and real God,
and be one with Him organically
in His Son Jesus Christ, who is eternal life to us.

The Anointing

Scripture Reading: 1 John 2:20, 27; Phil. 1:19; Exo. 30:22-33

Day 1 I. **The anointing is the moving and working of the indwelling compound Spirit to apply all the ingredients of the processed Triune God and His activities into our inner being so that we may be fully mingled with Him for His corporate expression (1 John 2:20, 27; cf. Eph. 4:4-6):**

A. The Triune God, after passing through the processes of incarnation, human living, crucifixion, resurrection, and ascension, has become the all-inclusive, life-giving compound Spirit (John 1:14; 1 Cor. 15:45b; Phil. 1:19).

B. He is within our spirit to anoint us, to "paint" us, with the elements of the Triune God; the more this anointing, this "painting," goes on, the more the Triune God with His person and processes is transfused into our being.

C. We need to be "painted" persons, those who are saturated with the anointing; we should be those on whom the paint is "wet," always having a fresh application of the all-inclusive Spirit as the divine paint so that we may paint others with the all-inclusive Spirit (Psa. 92:10; Zech. 4:14; 2 Cor. 3:6, 8).

D. By the anointing of the all-inclusive, compound Spirit, who is the composition of the Divine Trinity, we know and enjoy the Father, the Son, and the Spirit as our life and life supply (1 John 2:20, 27).

Day 2 II. **We need to see and experience the compounded ingredients of our abundantly rich processed and consummated Triune God, who is the anointing Spirit, typified by the holy anointing oil (Exo. 30:22-33):**

A. Olive oil signifies the Spirit of God with divinity;

the olive oil as the base of the compound ointment, the holy anointing oil, is produced by the
pressing of olives, signifying the Spirit of God
flowing out through the pressure of Christ's
death (Isa. 61:1-2; Heb. 1:9; Matt. 26:36).

B. Flowing myrrh signifies the precious death of
Christ:

1. Myrrh was used to reduce pain and heal the
body when it gave off the wrong kind of
secretion (Mark 15:23; John 19:39).

2. The Spirit was compounded through
Christ's sufferings in His living a crucified
life, a life of myrrh from the manger to
the cross, as the first God-man (Matt. 2:11;
John 19:39; Isa. 53:2-3).

3. The Spirit leads us to the cross, the cross is
applied by the Spirit, and the cross issues in
more abundance of the Spirit (Heb. 9:14;
Rom. 6:3, 6; 8:13-14; Gal. 2:20; John 12:24).

C. Sweet cinnamon signifies the sweetness and
effectiveness of Christ's death:

1. Cinnamon has a distinctive, sweet flavor
and can be used to stimulate a weak heart
(cf. Neh. 8:10; Isa. 42:4a).

2. We are conformed to the death of Christ by
our outward, consuming environment in
cooperation with the indwelling, crucifying
Spirit (2 Cor. 4:10-11, 16; Rom. 8:13-14; Gal.
5:24; 6:17; Col. 3:5).

D. Sweet calamus signifies the precious resurrection of Christ:

1. Calamus is a reed standing up (shooting
into the air) and growing in a marsh or
muddy place (cf. 1 Pet. 3:18).

2. We need to experience the Spirit as the
reality of Christ's resurrection (John 11:25;
20:22; Lam. 3:55-57).

E. Cassia signifies the repelling power of Christ's
resurrection:

1. Cassia was used as a repellent to drive away insects and snakes (cf. Eph. 6:10-11, 17b-18).
2. We need to know the power of Christ's resurrection in the life-giving Spirit as the all-sufficient grace of the processed and consummated Triune God (Phil. 3:10; 2 Cor. 12:9-10; 1 Cor. 15:10, 45b, 58; Phil. 4:23).

Day 3 III. **We need to see and experience the reality of the numbers used in the type of the holy anointing oil:**
  A. The only God is signified by the one hin of olive oil (Exo. 30:24; 1 Tim. 1:17).
  B. The Triune God—the Father, the Son, and the Spirit—is signified by the three units of the measure of the four spices (Exo. 30:23-24).

Day 4 C. Man, the creature of God, is signified by the four spices of the plant life (vv. 23-24; John 19:5; 1 Tim. 2:5).
  D. The mingling of divinity with humanity is typified by the blending of the olive oil with the four spices (Rom. 8:16; 1 Cor. 6:17).
  E. The power for responsibility is signified by the number five (Matt. 25:2, 4, 8).

Day 5 F. The building element is signified by the numbers three and five (Gen. 6:15-16; Exo. 26:3; 27:13-15).

  IV. **We need to see and be warned by the intrinsic significance of the prohibitions concerning the use of the holy anointing oil; this is to keep us from having a living that is in the principle of antichrist, the principle of being against Christ and replacing Christ, the principle of being "anti-anointing," which is to be "anti" the moving, working, and saturating of the Triune God within us (1 John 2:20-27; cf. Lev. 14:14-17):**

Day 6 A. The compound ointment was not to be poured upon the flesh of man—signifying that whenever we live and walk according to the flesh, we are through with the compound Spirit (Exo. 30:32; cf. Rom. 8:4; Gal. 5:16).

B. The compound ointment was not to be put upon a stranger—signifying that when we act and behave according to our flesh, we are in the old creation and are regarded as strangers in the sight of God (Exo. 30:33; Gal. 5:24-25).

C. The children of Israel were not to make anything like it, according to its composition—signifying that we should not imitate anything of the compound Spirit, any spiritual virtue, by the effort of our natural life (Exo. 30:32; cf. Matt. 15:7-8; Gal. 5:22-23).

V. **The holy anointing oil is solely for the purpose of anointing God's dwelling place and the priesthood; hence, only those who are for God's dwelling place and for the priesthood can have the enjoyment of the compound, all-inclusive Spirit as the anointing (Exo. 30:26-31; Phil. 1:19).**

VI. **The anointing of the compound, all-inclusive, life-giving Spirit is the element of our oneness for the building up of the Body of Christ in the divine dispensing of the Divine Trinity; the ground of oneness is simply the processed Triune God applied to our being (Psa. 133; Eph. 4:3-6).**

Morning Nourishment

1 John
2:20   And you have an anointing from the Holy One, and all of you know.

27   And as for you, the anointing which you have received from Him abides in you, and you have no need that anyone teach you; but as His anointing teaches you concerning all things and is true and is not a lie, and even as it has taught you, abide in Him.

First John 2:20 speaks not of the ointment but of the anointing. The word "anointing" denotes something experiential that is taking place within us. The anointing is the moving and working of the indwelling compound Spirit. This all-inclusive life-giving Spirit from the Holy One entered into us at the time of our regeneration and abides in us forever (v. 27).

Concerning the indwelling of the Divine Trinity (John 14:17, 23), we do not need anyone to teach us [1 John 2:27]. By the anointing of the all-inclusive compound Spirit, who is the composition of the Divine Trinity, we know and enjoy the Father, the Son, and the Spirit as our life and life supply.

According to verse 27, the anointing of the all-inclusive compound life-giving Spirit teaches us concerning all things. This is not an outward teaching by words, but an inward teaching by the anointing through our inner spiritual consciousness. This teaching by the anointing adds the divine elements of the Trinity, which are the elements of the anointing compound Spirit, into our inner being. It is like the repeated painting of some article: the paint not only gives color; its elements are also added to the thing painted, coat upon coat. It is in this way that the Triune God is transfused, infused, and added into all the inward parts of our being so that our inner man may grow in the divine life with the divine elements. (*Life-study of 1 John*, pp. 185, 200-201)

Today's Reading

God's intention is to work Himself into us as our life and our everything to make us His counterpart for the expression of Himself. In order to accomplish this, it was necessary for God to pass through the process of incarnation, human living, crucifixion, and resurrection. When He entered into resurrection, He became the compound, all-inclusive, life-giving Spirit. This Spirit is actually *Christos,* the anointed One, becoming the life-giving One. When we believed in the Lord Jesus, we received Him into us. The One we received is the anointed One, who through death and resurrection has become the anointing One. Furthermore, this anointing One is the all-inclusive indwelling Spirit. As soon as we believed in Him, He as the Spirit entered our spirit. Now He is within our spirit to anoint us, to "paint" us, with the element of the Triune God. The more this "painting" goes on, the more the element of the Triune God is transfused into our being. This is the anointing, which is the reality of the entire New Testament.

The anointing Spirit within is the consummation of the Triune God, and in this Spirit there are the elements of divinity, humanity, human living, crucifixion, and resurrection. He is the all-inclusive Spirit comprising all that God has accomplished, attained, and obtained. This Spirit is now the anointing One within us.

I am encouraged by the fact that many saints in the Lord's recovery, especially the young people, are enjoying this anointing. I expect that in the years to come the saints will go forth to preach and teach the wonderful, divine mysteries that are unknown to so many believers today. Many of us will be able to anoint others with the compound Spirit, applying this divine "paint" to them. If we would do this, we need to be "painted" persons, those who are saturated with the anointing. We should be those on whom the paint is "wet," always having a fresh application of the divine paint. Because this painting is taking place all the time, the paint on us should never dry. Then as such painted persons, we should go forth to paint others with the compound, all-inclusive, life-giving Spirit. (*Life-study of 1 John,* pp. 206, 209)

Further Reading: Life-study of 1 John, msgs. 22-24; *Life-study of Exodus,* msg. 166

Enlightenment and inspiration: _____

_____

_____

_____

Morning Nourishment

Exo.   **You also take the finest spices: of flowing myrrh five**
30:23-25 **hundred** *shekels,* **and of fragrant cinnamon half**
as much, two hundred fifty *shekels,* **and of fragrant**
calamus two hundred fifty *shekels,* **and of cassia**
five hundred *shekels,* **according to the shekel of the**
sanctuary, and a hin of olive oil. And you shall make
it a holy anointing oil, a fragrant ointment com-
pounded according to the work of a compounder;
it shall be a holy anointing oil.

In the Bible olive oil signifies the Spirit of God. Olive oil is produced by the pressing of olives. The olive oil signifies the Spirit of
God, through the pressure of Christ's death, flowing out.

The olive oil is the base of the ointment; it is the basic element
compounded with the spices. The four spices are compounded into
the olive oil to make the ointment. This indicates that the Spirit of
God, signified by the olive oil, is no longer merely oil, but now it is
oil compounded with certain ingredients. Regarding this, John 7:39
says, "But this He said concerning the Spirit, whom those who
believed into Him were about to receive; for the Spirit was not yet,
because Jesus had not yet been glorified." This means that before
the Lord's glorification, the compound Spirit was not yet. It was
after Christ's resurrection that the compounding, or the blending,
of such a Spirit was completed. (*Life-study of Exodus,* p. 1689)

Today's Reading

Flowing myrrh, smelling sweet but tasting bitter, signifies the
precious death of Christ. In the Bible...myrrh is related to death.
According to John 19, when Nicodemus and others were preparing to bury the body of the Lord Jesus, they used myrrh.

Myrrh comes from [the juice of] an aromatic tree....In ancient
times, this juice was used to reduce the suffering of death. When
the Lord Jesus was being crucified, He was offered wine mixed
with myrrh to reduce His pain. However, He refused to take it. No
doubt, the myrrh in Exodus 30 is a symbol of the Lord's death.

The aromatic liquid of myrrh...also can be used for healing

the body when it gives off the wrong kind of secretion....In our human life there are many wrong secretions, but the Lord's death on the cross corrects this problem.

Fragrant cinnamon signifies the sweetness and effectiveness of Christ's death. Cinnamon not only has a distinctive flavor, but it can also be used to stimulate the heart. Cinnamon may be prescribed to stimulate a weak heart.

Myrrh signifies the precious death of Christ, and cinnamon signifies the effectiveness of His death. If we apply the Lord's death to our situation, it will reduce our pain, correct the wrong secretions, and eventually stimulate us and make us happy and joyful. I can testify of this from my experience. There are times that negative things in my environment would cause me to be low. But when I apply the Lord's death, I am corrected, adjusted, stimulated, and stirred up.

The calamus in Exodus 30 is a reed....Calamus grows in a marsh or muddy place. But...it is able to shoot up into the air. According to the sequence of the spices, this calamus signifies the rising up of the Lord Jesus from the place of death....In resurrection [Christ] rose up and stood up. Calamus, therefore, signifies the precious resurrection of Christ.

The fourth spice, cassia, signifies the power of Christ's resurrection. Cassia and cinnamon belong to the same family. Cinnamon is from the inner part of the bark, and cassia, from the outer part of the bark. Both cinnamon and cassia are sweet and fragrant. Furthermore, the plants from which they are derived often live and grow in places where other plants cannot grow.

In ancient times cassia was used as a repellent to drive away insects and snakes. Cassia thus signifies the power, the effectiveness, of Christ's resurrection. Christ's resurrection can withstand any kind of environment, and His resurrection certainly is a repellent. It repels all evil "insects" and especially the old serpent, the devil. (*Life-study of Exodus*, pp. 1687-1689)

Further Reading: Life-study of Exodus, msgs. 157-162; *The Spirit*, ch. 12

Enlightenment and inspiration: _____

_____

_____

_____

Morning Nourishment

**Matt. Go therefore and disciple all the nations, baptiz-
28:19 ing them into the name of the Father and of the
Son and of the Holy Spirit.**

What are the ingredients, the elements, that constitute the
compound Spirit? The first element is the only God, the unique
God, signified both by the olive oil itself and also by the quantity
of olive oil, a hin,...a complete unit....The one hin of olive oil in
Exodus 30 signifies the only God, the Creator (1 Tim. 1:17; Rom.
16:27; Exo. 30:24).

One hin of olive oil as the base of the compounded ointment
signifies the unique God as the base of the compound Spirit....We
believe in God, but not in the simple way of the Jews....In the
New Testament God is no longer merely God with the single element of divinity, for He has been mingled with other elements.

Consider again the blending of the spices with the olive oil to
produce the compounded ointment. First, the olive oil was of one
element. But after it was compounded, or blended, with four
kinds of spices, it no longer had just a single element. It had
become a compound of five elements. Of these five elements,
one—the oil—is the base, and the others—the four spices—are
the ingredients for compounding. This indicates that in the Old
Testament the Spirit of God was of one element, and that element
was the unique God, the Creator. However, the New Testament
reveals that a process of blending, of compounding, has taken
place. This process involved Christ's incarnation, human living,
crucifixion, resurrection, and ascension. After passing through
this process of blending, compounding, the Spirit of God is no
longer simply the Spirit with one element. Now He is the compound Spirit. However, this Spirit still has the unique God as
the base. This base, the one God, is typified by the hin of olive oil.
(*Life-study of Exodus,* pp. 1743-1744)

Today's Reading

In the compound Spirit we also have the Triune God, the
Father, the Son, and the Spirit....In this ointment the Triune God

is typified by the three units of the measure of the four spices (Exo. 30:23-24). In the compounded ointment there were five hundred shekels of myrrh, two hundred fifty shekels each of cinnamon and calamus, and five hundred shekels of cassia. Although there were four spices, there was a total of three units of five hundred shekels in measure. But how can we apply this to the Triune God?...The second unit of five hundred shekels is split in half....Surely this points to the second of the Triune God, the Son, and to His crucifixion.

The greatest teaching in the Bible is that of the Trinity of the Godhead. According to the Hebrew language, the first time God is mentioned in the Bible (Gen. 1:1), the word *Elohim* is used. The name *Elohim,* meaning God, is in the plural. This is a hint of the Trinity. Furthermore, we are told in Genesis 1:26 that when God was about to create man, He said to Himself, "Let Us make man in Our image, according to Our likeness." This is another indication that God is triune. However, it is not, of course, a clear revelation of the Trinity. We have such a clear revelation in Matthew 28:19, where, after His resurrection, the Lord Jesus gave this charge to His disciples: "Go therefore and disciple all the nations, baptizing them into the name of the Father and of the Son and of the Holy Spirit." Here we have one name for the three of the Godhead, for the Father, the Son, and the Spirit.

Returning to the three units of five hundred shekels each in the compounded ointment, we see that it was the middle unit that was split in half. This signifies the putting to death of the Lord Jesus on the cross. The cutting into two pieces of the second unit of five hundred shekels points to the death of Christ. The fact that it was the middle unit, signifying the Son, that was split is a strong indication that these three units of five hundred shekels signify the Trinity....To have this understanding of the three units is to decipher the heavenly language in Exodus 30. (*Life-study of Exodus,* pp. 1744, 1746)

Further Reading: Life-study of Exodus, msgs. 163, 165

Enlightenment and inspiration: _____
_____
_____
_____

Morning Nourishment

Exo.   You also take the finest spices: of flowing myrrh
30:23-24   five hundred *shekels,* and of fragrant cinnamon
half as much, two hundred fifty *shekels,* and of fragrant calamus two hundred fifty *shekels,* and of
cassia five hundred *shekels...*

1 Tim.   For there is one God and one Mediator of God and
2:5   men, the man Christ Jesus.

1 Cor.   But he who is joined to the Lord is one spirit.
6:17

Next in the ingredients of the compound Spirit we have
man, the creature of God. This, of course, refers to the humanity of Jesus, or to the man Jesus....man is typified by the four
spices of the plant life (Exo. 30:23-24).

The number four in the Bible signifies God's creation. A strong
proof of this is the four living creatures in Ezekiel and Revelation.
In Revelation 4 John explicitly mentions four living creatures....
The leading one among the four living creatures has the face of a
man. This indicates that man is the leading one of God's creation,
a fact that corresponds to Genesis 1. Although God created man
last, God made him to be the head over creation. God gave man
the dominion to rule all His creatures. In Exodus 30 man is signified by the four spices.

Let us now consider two verses in the New Testament related
to the humanity of Christ. John 19:5 gives a word uttered by
Pilate shortly before the Lord was crucified: "Then Jesus came
out, wearing the thorny crown and the purple garment. And he
said to them, Behold, the man!" First Timothy 2:5 says, "For there
is one God and one Mediator of God and men, the man Christ
Jesus." This word was written by Paul after the Lord's ascension.
Paul's statement reveals that even after His crucifixion, resurrection, and ascension, the Lord Jesus is still a man. (*Life-study of
Exodus,* pp. 1746-1747)

Today's Reading

The mingling of divinity with humanity is typified by the
blending of the olive oil with the four spices. We have seen that

the olive oil signifies the unique God and that the four spices signify man as the leading one in God's creation. Therefore, the mingling of God and man is typified by the blending of the oil and spices.

Do not listen to those who say that there is not such a thing in the Bible as the mingling of divinity with humanity. There is a clear revelation of this matter in the Word. In Exodus 30 we have a type of the mingling, but in the New Testament we have the fulfillment. The fulfillment of the type is the mingling of the divine Spirit with our regenerated human spirit. Romans 8:16 says, "The Spirit Himself witnesses with our spirit that we are children of God." Here we see the mingling of the Spirit with our spirit. Furthermore, 1 Corinthians 6:17 says, "He who is joined to the Lord is one spirit." This proves that our spirit has been joined to, mingled with, the Spirit.

The power for responsibility is also an element in the compound Spirit. I can testify that when I walk in the all-inclusive Spirit, I have the power to bear responsibility....The fact that the compound Spirit typified by the compounded ointment contains the element of power for responsibility is indicated by the five elements of the compounded ointment and the three times five hundred shekels of the four spices. In the Bible five is the number of responsibility (Matt. 25:4, 8). The number five is seen in the five elements of the compounded ointment. As we pointed out in the previous message, we see the number three signifying the Triune God, with the three units of five hundred shekels of the four spices. The middle unit is split in half and signifies the cutting of the Lord Jesus on the cross. Furthermore, the number three signifies resurrection. After the cutting, we have the calamus signifying resurrection. Therefore, here the number three signifies the Triune God in resurrection. When we experience the compound Spirit, the Triune God in resurrection becomes our portion. This is the power, the capability, for bearing responsibility. (*Life-study of Exodus*, pp. 1752-1753)

Further Reading: Life-study of Exodus, msg. 164

Enlightenment and inspiration: _____

_____

_____

Morning Nourishment

Gen. **And this is how you shall make it: The length of the**
6:15-16 **ark shall be three hundred cubits, its width fifty
cubits, and its height thirty cubits....You shall make
it with lower, second, and third *stories*.**

1 John **Who is the liar if not he who denies that Jesus is the**
2:22 **Christ? This is the antichrist, the one who denies
the Father and the Son.**

The numbers three and five indicate that the building element is also included in the compound Spirit. Here we have three complete units of five hundred shekels each....Furthermore, we have the five elements, the olive oil and the four spices.

According to the Old Testament, the numbers three and five are related to God's building. The first building of God was the ark made by Noah....With the dimensions of the ark we have multiples of the numbers three and five [Gen. 6:15]. Moreover,...the ark was to be made with "lower, second, and third stories" [v. 16].

The tabernacle was of three sections: the outer court, the Holy Place, and the Holy of Holies. According to Exodus 27, [many of the measurements related to the...tabernacle were composed of the numbers three and five.]

If we believe that everything in the Bible has a significance, then we should believe that the numbers three and five signify something. A careful study of the Word shows that these numbers are related to God's building. Therefore, in the compound Spirit we have the Triune God in resurrection mingled with His creature, man, for the power to bear responsibility, and we also have the element for God's building.

Altogether we have ten ingredients, giving us a full portrait of the compound Spirit. In the compound Spirit we have the unique God, the Triune God, the man Jesus, the death of Christ, the effectiveness of the death of Christ, the resurrection of Christ, the power of Christ's resurrection, the mingling of divinity with humanity, the power for responsibility, and the element of God's building. All these are ingredients of the compound Spirit. (*Life-study of Exodus*, pp. 1753-1754)

Today's Reading

The Greek prefix *anti* has two main meanings. First, it means against; second, it means in place of, or instead of. This indicates that an antichrist is against Christ and also replaces Christ with something else. To be an antichrist is, on the one hand, to be against Christ; on the other hand, it is also to have something instead of Christ, something that replaces Christ....The principle of antichrist involves denying what Christ is....Whenever someone denies what Christ is, automatically that person will replace Christ with something else. Hence, an antichrist is both against Christ and is one who replaces Christ.

One may not be against Christ or deny Christ consciously. But unconsciously we may deny some aspect of Christ's person and then replace this aspect with something else.

We all need to apply this word to ourselves and be on the alert lest in any way we follow the principle of antichrist. If we deny an aspect of Christ's person, we are against Him, anti Him. If we have something in our daily living that replaces Christ, we also are against Christ, anti Christ. To be anti Christ is both to be against Christ and to replace Christ with something else. If we replace Christ with our own good character and behavior, we are practicing the principle of antichrist. In a practical way, we are against the anointing, anti the moving, working, and saturating of the Triune God within us. Instead of being anti the anointing, we must live according to the anointing. Otherwise, we shall be against Christ or we shall replace Christ with something else.

We may follow the principle of antichrist in our daily living... [by replacing] Christ with things of our culture and our natural life....Whatever our race or culture may be, we may replace Christ with our culture or with our way of having our daily life according to our culture. To replace Christ in this way is to practice the principle of antichrist. (*Life-study of 1 John*, pp. 272-273, 295-296)

Further Reading: Life-study of 1 John, msgs. 31-33

Enlightenment and inspiration: _____

_____

_____

_____

Morning Nourishment

Exo. Upon the flesh of man it shall not be poured, nor
30:32-33 shall you make *any* like it, according to its composition; it is holy, *and* it shall be holy to you. Whoever
compounds *any* like it or whoever puts any of it
upon a stranger, he shall be cut off from his people.
26 And with it you shall anoint the Tent of Meeting
and the Ark of the Testimony.
30 And you shall anoint Aaron and his sons and sanctify them that they may serve Me as priests.

[Concerning the holy anointing oil], Exodus 30:32 says that
"upon the flesh of man it shall not be poured." In the Bible the
flesh of man denotes fallen man in the old creation....The command not to pour the anointing oil upon the flesh of man indicates
that the anointing is not to be applied to men of the old creation.
Whenever we live and walk according to the flesh, we are through
with the Spirit of Christ. If we would partake of this Spirit and
enjoy the all-inclusive Spirit, we must remain in our spirit.

The Spirit of Christ cannot be poured upon our old nature, our
old man. Our flesh does not have the position to participate in this
compound ointment. Whenever you lose your temper, you are in
the flesh and cannot enjoy the Spirit of Christ. But whenever you
turn to your spirit, immediately in your spirit you sense the
anointing. You realize that you are being painted with the Spirit
of Christ, for you are in the new creation, not in your old nature.
(*Life-study of Exodus,* p. 1695)

Today's Reading

Exodus 30:33 indicates that the ointment was not to be put
upon a stranger. The word "stranger" implies a comparison
between those who are priests and those who are not. The priests
serving in the presence of God do not act according to the old
nature. Instead, they live according to their new nature and
thereby enjoy the anointing. However, in the sight of God all other
people are strangers. We may say that the flesh, the old man, is a
stranger. We Christians today are not strangers; we are priests.

...We must remain in our spirit, and we must live, act, speak, and contact others in the spirit. Then we shall be in the new creation as priests serving God and participating in the Spirit of Christ. The command not to make anything like the anointing oil in its proportions means that we should not imitate it [vv. 32-33]. However, among Christians today there is a great deal of imitation. Therefore, we need to discern what is truly of the Spirit and what is an imitation. For example, a person's humility may not be of the Spirit. In China I saw some disciples of Confucius who were much more humble than many Christian teachers. But that humility had nothing to do with the Spirit of Christ....Many Christians try to act humble. This humility, however, is not of the Spirit of Christ. Rather, it is an imitation.

Do not imitate any spiritual virtue by your own effort. To do this is to make something like the ointment. In the sight of God this is an abomination....Our honesty,...our love, humility, patience, and kindness—indeed, every virtue—must be a product of the indwelling Spirit. Otherwise, we are imitating the ointment....Therefore, we should not act in our old nature and we should not imitate anything that is of the Spirit of Christ.

The function of the compound Spirit is to anoint the dwelling place of God with its furniture and utensils (Exo. 30:26-29) and to anoint the priesthood of God (30:30). This indicates that the compound Spirit is for God's building and for His priesthood. If we are not for God's building and priesthood, we cannot have any share in the compound Spirit, although we may have some enjoyment of and participation in the Spirit of God, the Spirit of the Lord, and the Holy Spirit. Only those who are for the building of God and the priesthood of God can have the enjoyment of the compound, all-inclusive, processed Spirit. All the ingredients, all the rich elements, of the compound Spirit are for God's house and God's priesthood. (*Life-study of Exodus,* pp. 1695-1697, 1731-1732)

Further Reading: The Genuine Ground of Oneness, pp. 83-86; *The Experience of Christ as Life for the Building Up of the Church,* chs. 10-11

Enlightenment and inspiration: _____

_____

_____

_____

Hymns, #1116

1   Pure myrrh and cinnamon,
Calamus and cassia—
These are Thy elements,
    Jesus my Lord!
In olive oil they're blent
In wondrous measurement—
O what an ointment this,
    Anointing us!

Four-in-one mingled,
Compounded Spirit,
Sweet with Christ's suffering death,
Full of the fragrance
Of resurrection—
O what an ointment flows
    In spirit, Lord!

2   Stacte and onycha,
Galbanum and frankincense—
These are Thy elements,
    Jesus my Lord!
Stacte doth sons produce,
Onycha from sin doth loose,
Galbanum all death repels,
    In spirit, Lord.

Equal proportion,
In resurrection;
Seasoned with salt are they.
Ground into powder fine,
Consumed with fire divine—
O what an incense this,
    Jesus my Lord!

3   Ointment is Christ for us,
Exceeding glorious!
Incense is Christ for God,
    Wholly for Him.
Ointment flows down to us,
Christ is our portion thus;
Incense ascends to God,
    Fragrant to Him.

'Tis by th' anointing
Christ we experience
And then the incense burn.
Christ in our prayer and praise—
O what a Christ we raise
From our experience,
    Precious to God.

Composition for prophecy with main point and sub-points: _____

_____

_____

_____

_____

_____

_____

_____

_____

_____

_____

_____

_____

_____

_____

_____

_____

_____

_____

_____

_____

_____

_____

_____

_____

_____

_____

_____

_____

_____

_____

_____

Abiding in Christ

Scripture Reading: John 14:23; 15:4-5; 1 John 2:27-28; 3:24; 4:13; Rev. 21:3, 22

Day 1
&
Day 2

I. **To abide in Christ is to dwell in Him, to remain in fellowship with Him, that we may experience and enjoy His abiding in us (John 15:4-5; 1 John 2:27):**

A. To abide in Christ is to live in the Divine Trinity—taking Christ as our dwelling place (vv. 6, 24, 27-28; 3:6, 24; 4:13):

1. To abide in Christ is to abide in the Son and in the Father (2:24); this is to remain and dwell in the Lord (John 15:4-5).

2. To abide in Christ is to abide in the fellowship of the divine life and to walk in the divine light, that is, to abide in the divine light (1 John 1:2-3, 6-7; 2:10).

B. To have Christ abiding in us is to live with the Divine Trinity—having Christ's presence as our enjoyment for Him to be one with us and to be with every part of our being and every aspect of our living (Matt. 1:23; 18:20; 28:20; 2 Tim. 4:22; 2 Cor. 2:10; 1 Cor. 7:24):

1. To have Christ abiding in us is to have the words of Christ abiding in us for the bearing of remaining fruit to glorify the Father (John 15:7-8, 16).

2. To have Christ abiding in us is to have the Spirit of reality as the presence of the Triune God abiding in us (14:17).

Day 3

II. **We need to abide in Christ as our King and as our royal abode so that He can abide in us to make us His queen and His royal palace, His glorious church (Psa. 45:13, 8; John 15:4-5; Eph. 5:27; Rev. 22:5; Rom. 5:17; cf. S. S. 6:4):**

A. To abide in Christ is to dwell in Him, the eternal God, as our Lord, having our living in Him and taking Him as our everything (John 15:4-5; 1 John 4:15-16; Rev. 21:22; Deut. 33:27a; Psa. 90).

B. We need to dwell in God, living in Him every minute, for outside of Him there are sins and afflictions (vv. 3-11; John 16:33).

C. To take God as our habitation, our eternal dwelling place, is the highest and fullest experience of God (Psa. 91).

Day 4 III. **To abide in Christ, taking Him as our dwelling place, and to allow Him to abide in us, taking us as His dwelling place, is to live in the reality of the universal incorporation of the processed and consummated Triune God with the redeemed and regenerated believers (John 14:2, 10-11, 17, 20, 23):**

A. The New Jerusalem is the ultimate incorporation of the processed and consummated Triune God with the regenerated, sanctified, renewed, transformed, conformed, and glorified tripartite church (Rev. 21:3, 22).

B. The New Jerusalem is the tabernacle of God, and the center of the tabernacle is Christ as the hidden manna; the way to be incorporated into this universal, divine-human incorporation, the mutual abode of God and man, is to eat Christ as the hidden manna (v. 3; Exo. 16:32-34; Heb. 9:4; Rev. 2:17).

Day 5 IV. **We abide in Christ so that He may abide in us by loving Him (John 14:21, 23):**

A. When we love the Lord Jesus, He manifests Himself to us, and the Father comes with Him to make an abode with us for our enjoyment; this abode is a mutual abode, in which the Triune God abides in us and we abide in Him (v. 23).

B. The more we love the Lord, the more we shall have His presence, and the more we are in His presence, the more we shall enjoy all that He is to us; the Lord's recovery is a recovery of loving the Lord Jesus (1 Cor. 2:9-10; Eph. 6:24).

V. **We abide in Christ so that He may abide in us by caring for the inward teaching of the all-inclusive anointing (1 John 2:27):**

A. We abide in the divine fellowship with Christ by experiencing the cleansing of the Lord's blood and the application of the anointing Spirit to our inner being (John 15:4-5; 1 John 1:5, 7; 2:20, 27).

B. Christ as the Head is the anointed One and the anointing One, and we are His members enjoying Him as the inner anointing for the fulfillment of His purpose (Heb. 1:9; 3:14; 2 Cor. 1:21-22).

C. The anointing, as the moving and working of the compound Spirit within us, anoints God into us so that we may be saturated with God, possess God, and understand the mind of God; the anointing communicates the mind of Christ as the Head of the Body to His members by the inner sense, the inner consciousness, of life (Psa. 133; 1 Cor. 2:16; Rom. 8:6, 27).

D. When the Head wants a member of the Body to move, He intimates it through the inner anointing, and as we yield to the anointing, life flows freely from the Head to us; if we resist the anointing, our relationship with the Head is interfered with, and the flow of life within us is stopped (Col. 2:19).

E. The teaching of the anointing of the Spirit has nothing to do with right or wrong; it is an inner sense of life (Acts 16:6-7; 2 Cor. 2:13).

F. If our natural life is dealt with by the cross and if we submit to the headship of Christ and live the Body life, we will have the Spirit's anointing and enjoy the fellowship of the Body (Eph. 4:3-6, 15-16).

Day 6 VI. **We abide in Christ so that He may abide in us by "switching on" the law of the Spirit of life in our spirit (Rom. 8:2, 4):**

A. The Lord's abiding in us and our abiding in Him
are altogether a matter of Him being the life-
giving Spirit in our spirit; by the bountiful,
immeasurable Spirit in our spirit, we know with
full assurance that we and God are one and that
we abide in each other (1 Cor. 15:45b; Rom. 8:16;
1 Cor. 6:17; Phil. 1:19; John 3:34; 1 John 3:24;
4:13).

B. The way to abide in Christ as the empowering
One so that He may be activated within us as
the inner operating God, the law of the Spirit of
life, is by rejoicing always, praying unceasingly,
and giving thanks in everything (Phil. 4:13;
2:13; 1 Thes. 5:16-18; Col. 3:17).

VII. **We abide in Christ so that He may abide in
us by dealing with the constant word in the
Scriptures, which is outside of us, and
the present word as the Spirit, which is within us (John 5:39-40; 6:63; 2 Cor. 3:6; Rev. 2:7):**

A. By the outward, written word we have the
explanation, definition, and expression of the
mysterious Lord, and by the inward, living word
we have the experience of the abiding Christ
and the presence of the practical Lord (Eph.
5:26; 6:17-18).

B. If we abide in the Lord's constant and written
word, His instant and living words will abide in
us (John 8:31; 15:7; 1 John 2:14).

C. We abide in Him and His words abide in us so
that we may speak in Him and He may speak in
us for the building of God into man and man into
God (John 15:7; 2 Cor. 2:17; 13:3; 1 Cor. 14:4b).

Morning Nourishment

1 John   ...Whatever we ask we receive from Him because we
3:22-24   keep His commandments and do the things that are
          pleasing in His sight. And this is His commandment,
          that we believe in the name of His Son Jesus Christ and
          love one another, even as He gave a commandment
          to us. And he who keeps His commandments abides
          in Him, and He in him. And in this we know that He
          abides in us, by the Spirit whom He gave to us.

The Lord Jesus told us in John 15[:4-5] that He is the vine and
that we are the branches of the vine. As the branches of the vine
we should abide in Him. Then He will abide in us. To abide in Christ
is to live in Christ, and to live in Christ is to live in the Divine
Trinity. To have Christ abide in us is to have the Triune God living
in us. This is to live with the Divine Trinity....John is a book on
living in and with the Divine Trinity,...[and] in the Epistles we
can see all the practicalities and details of living in and with the
Divine Trinity. We need to be brought into the experiences of living in the Divine Trinity and with the Divine Trinity. When we
abide in Him, we live in Him. When we have Him abide in us,
we live with Him. (*Living in and with the Divine Trinity,* p. 79)

Today's Reading

We need to be those abiding in the Lord (1 John 2:6). To abide
in the Triune God is to abide in the Lord. The Lord is the One who
possesses all things, who rules over all things, who exercises His
sovereignty over all things and over all people. We are living in
the One who is the Lord of this universe. If we are not obedient to
Him or do not subject ourselves to Him, that will annul our abiding in Him. To abide in Christ is to abide in the Lord.

We also need to be those abiding in the Son (1 John 2:24b)....
The Son is the One who possesses the Father's life with the Father's
nature to express the Father. The sons have the full right to enjoy
all the privileges and rights ascribed to the sonship. When we are
abiding in the Son, we enjoy our Father's life, our Father's nature,
and the privilege, the right, to express Him and to enjoy all His

possessions. To abide in the Lord concerns the lordship of Christ. To abide in the Son concerns the sonship of Christ.

We also need to be those who are abiding in the Father (1 John 2:24c). How good it is to have a Father! Our Father is all capable. Our Father is always living....He takes care of us in every way and in everything....We are not only abiding in Christ as the organism of the Triune God, in the Lord with His lordship, and in the Son with His sonship, but also in the Father with all His care.

Our abiding in the Son and in the Father are both mentioned in 1 John 2:24. When we have the Son, we have the Father because the Son and the Father are one. The Father is in the Son, and the Son is in the Father (John 14:10). When we abide in the Son, we abide in the Father....We have the Lord and we have the Father. We have the Son with the Father. When we abide in the Son, we enjoy the fatherhood because the Father is there.

We also need to be those who are abiding in God (1 John 3:24a). All these different titles—the Lord, the Son, the Father, and God—bear some significance. In order to understand what it means to abide in God, we need to read 1 John 3:22-24....God is the One who gave the commandments. These commandments are that we have to believe in His Son and that we have to love one another. We need to have the faith in Jesus Christ, the Son of God, and we need to have the love to love all the brothers. This is what it means to abide in God....This is to have faith and love.

In 1 John we see that we need to abide in the Lord, in the Son, in the Father, and in God. This presents a full portrait of living in the Triune God. To live in the Triune God is to have a daily life in Christ as the organism of the Triune God, in the Lord with His headship, with His lordship, in the Son with His sonship, in the Father with His fatherhood, and in God with His commandments of believing in His Son and of loving all His other sons. This is what it means to experience the Divine Trinity in our daily life. (*Living in and with the Divine Trinity*, pp. 83-85)

Further Reading: Living in and with the Divine Trinity, chs. 4, 8-9

Enlightenment and inspiration: _____

_____

_____

Morning Nourishment

1 John As for you, that which you heard from the begin-
2:24 ning, let it abide in you. If that which you heard
from the beginning abides in you, you also will
abide in the Son and in the Father.

John *Even* the Spirit of reality, whom the world cannot
14:17 receive, because it does not behold Him or know
Him; but you know Him, because He abides with
you and shall be in you.

To live in the Divine Trinity is to abide in Christ, and to live with the Divine Trinity is to have Christ abide in us (John 15:5). When we abide in Christ, Christ abides in us, and His abiding is His presence with us. When He abides in us, we have His presence. We have Him with us for our enjoyment.

To have Christ abiding in us is to have the words of Christ abiding in us for the bearing of remaining fruit (John 15:7-8, 16). In John 15:7 the Lord said, "If you abide in Me and My words abide in you, ask whatever you will, and it shall be done for you." This kind of asking is related to fruit-bearing (v. 8) and surely will be fulfilled. If we are to be those who go forth to preach the gospel, we must be those who love the word of Christ. We must be those who have the living word, the word of life, abiding in us. If we are not such persons, our preaching of the gospel will not last long. The living word of Christ stirs us up to go forth and bear fruit. The word of Christ abiding in us brings us the enjoyment of all that the Triune God is. This encourages us, stirs us up, burdens us, and charges us to go forth to preach the gospel to people. (*Living in and with the Divine Trinity,* pp. 100-101)

Today's Reading

If we do not have the word of Christ abiding in us, we may go out to reach people, but what we do will be in a poor way. The content and the issue of what we do will be vain, empty. If we are going to do a rich work, a work full of the riches of the

Triune God, we must have the word of Christ abiding in us. Then when we talk to people, we will not talk to them with our own opinion, our own thought, our own word, our own expression, or our own utterance. We will talk to people with the word of Christ. This is why Paul charges us in Colossians 3:16 to let the word of Christ abide in us richly. We need to have a storage of the word of Christ in us. Then what we speak will be the word of Christ, which expresses the very riches of Christ. To have the word of Christ abide in us is a rich enjoyment of the Triune God.

To have Christ abiding in us is to have the Spirit of reality abiding in us (John 14:17). John 14—16 is a long message given by the Lord just before He was betrayed. In chapter fifteen the Lord mentions His words abiding in us, and in chapter fourteen He speaks of the Spirit of reality abiding in us. Actually, the words of Christ and the Spirit of reality are one. In John 6:63 the Lord told us that the words which He has spoken are spirit. God's word and God the Spirit are both God's breath. When this breath gets into us and remains in us, this breath is the Spirit. When this breath comes out of us through our speaking, it becomes the word. When we breathe in the word of the Bible, the word becomes the Spirit in us. We contact our Triune God through the Spirit and in the word. We enjoy Him through the Spirit in our spirit and in the word. As long as we have His words abiding in us, this issues in the Spirit abiding in us. The more His words abide in us, the more the Spirit abides in us. These are two aspects of the breath of our Triune God.

First John 3:24a speaks of God abiding in us. The word, the Spirit, and God are one. Both the word and the Spirit are the reality of the Triune God. The word is the Spirit, and the Spirit is God. These three are one for our enjoyment. (*Living in and with the Divine Trinity,* pp. 101-102)

Further Reading: Living in and with the Divine Trinity, ch. 10

Enlightenment and inspiration: _____

_____

_____

_____

Morning Nourishment

Psa. **O Lord, You have been our dwelling place / In all gen-**
90:1 **erations.**
91:1 **He who dwells in the secret place of the Most High /**
Will abide in the shadow of the Almighty.
   9 **For You have made Jehovah,** *who is* **my refuge, /** *Even*
the Most High, Your habitation.

To abide in Christ is to dwell in Him, not just remain or stay in
Him. When we dwell in our house, we have our life and our living
there. This means that our life and living are altogether wrapped
up with our dwelling place.

According to Moses' word in Psalm 90:1, our house, our dwelling place, is the Triune God as our Lord....When we experience
the Triune God to the degree that we take Him as our dwelling
place, we have the deeper experience of God.

Psalm 91:11 and 12 indicate that "You" and "Your" in verse 9
refer to Christ. These verses are quoted in Matthew 4:6 and applied
to Christ. This reveals that not only Moses took God as his dwelling place, but even the Lord Jesus, while He was on earth, took
God the Father as His habitation. Moses, the lawgiver, and Christ,
the grace-giver, were the same in taking God as their dwelling
place, as their habitation. (*Life-study of the Psalms,* pp. 399-400)

Today's Reading

To take God as our habitation, our dwelling place, is the highest and fullest experience of God. To take God as our dwelling
place is to experience Him to the fullest extent. Probably no one
among us would dare to say that he dwells in God all the time.
But this is what Christ did. When He was living His human life
on earth, He continually took God the Father as His habitation.

To be identified with Christ is to be identified with Him not
only in His death, in His resurrection, and in His ascension but
also in His taking God as His habitation. We are identified with
Christ to such an extent....If we would be identified with Christ,
...we need to abide in Christ. If we do not abide in Christ, we are
separated from Him and thus are not identified with Him. The

only way that we can be identified with Christ in His death, resurrection, and ascension is to abide in Christ, and to abide in Christ is not only to remain in Him but also to dwell in Him, taking Him as our everything.

If you take God as your dwelling place, you will realize that the span of your life on earth is short (Psa. 90: 3-11). In verse 10 Moses said, "The days of our years are seventy years, / Or, if because of strength, eighty years; / But their pride is labor and sorrow, / For it is soon gone, and we fly away." With the Lord, however, a thousand years are "like yesterday when it passes by and like a watch in the night" (v. 4). According to the Bible,…Methuselah…lived nine hundred sixty-nine years. In the sight of God, however, this was less than a day. The short span of our life is full of sins and afflictions. If one has such a realization, he must be one who takes God as his dwelling place. I want to dwell in God, living in Him every minute, for outside of Him there are sins and afflictions.

In the identification with Christ, the saints make Jehovah the Most High their habitation, dwelling in His secret place and abiding in His shadow under His wings (91:1-9). We all need to dwell in God by dwelling in the secret place (v. 1). This is the real oneness with God. Here God becomes us; we are constituted with Him; and we and God live together as one.

Psalm 92:12 through 14 says, "The righteous man will flourish like the palm tree; / He will grow like a cedar in Lebanon. / Planted in the house of Jehovah, / They will flourish in the courts of our God. / They will still bring forth fruit in old age; / They will be full of sap and green." The poetry here is a picture of those who experience God in a deeper way by dwelling in Him, taking Him as everything in their living in the house of God. (*Life-study of the Psalms,* pp. 400, 402-403, 405)

Further Reading: Life-study of the Psalms, msg. 35; *Christ and the Church Revealed and Typified in the Psalms,* ch. 16; *The Application of the Interpretation of the New Jerusalem to the Seeking Believers,* msg. 4; *Crystallization-study of Song of Songs,* msg. 11*

Enlightenment and inspiration: _____

_____

_____

Morning Nourishment

Rev. And I heard a loud voice out of the throne, saying,
21:3 Behold, the tabernacle of God is with men...
22 And I saw no temple in it, for the Lord God the
Almighty and the Lamb are its temple.
2:17 ...To him who overcomes, to him I will give of the
hidden manna...

I have spent more than seventy years studying the Bible, but only very recently did I see that the Bible actually unveils just one thing—the universal incorporation.

Although we have seen that the New Jerusalem is the goal of God's economy, we did not see that the New Jerusalem is an incorporation. In Revelation 21:2 the apostle John says, "I saw the holy city, New Jerusalem," and in the next verse he speaks of the New Jerusalem as "the tabernacle of God." As the tabernacle of God the New Jerusalem is God's dwelling place. We are quite familiar with this aspect of the New Jerusalem; it has become old knowledge to us. Now we need to learn something new and see that as the tabernacle of God the New Jerusalem is the universal incorporation.

As part of His promise to the overcomer in Pergamos, the Lord Jesus said, "To him who overcomes, to him I will give of the hidden manna" (2:17)....Manna is a type of Christ as the heavenly food that enables God's people to go His way. A portion of manna was preserved in a golden pot concealed in the Ark (Exo. 16:32-34; Heb. 9:4). This hidden manna, signifying the hidden Christ, is a special portion reserved for His overcoming believers, who overcome the degradation of the worldly church. While the church goes the way of the world, these overcomers come forward to abide in the Holy of Holies, where they enjoy the hidden Christ as a special portion for their daily supply. (*The Issue of Christ Being Glorified by the Father with the Divine Glory*, pp. 29-30)

Today's Reading

Now we come to a crucial matter: To eat the hidden manna is to be incorporated into the tabernacle. The tabernacle in the Old Testament is a sign of the universal incorporation. Christ as the hidden manna is the center of the tabernacle. The hidden manna is in the golden pot; the golden pot is in the Ark, made of acacia wood overlaid with gold; and this Ark is in the Holy of Holies. The hidden manna, which signifies Christ, is in the golden pot, which refers to God. The manna in the golden pot indicates that Christ is in the Father (John 14:10a, 11a). The Ark is in the Holy of Holies, and the Holy of Holies is our spirit. Today, our spirit indwelt by the Holy Spirit is the Holy of Holies. From this we can see that Christ as the hidden manna is in God the Father as the golden pot; that the Father is in Christ as the Ark with His two natures, divinity and humanity; and that this Christ as the indwelling Spirit lives in our regenerated spirit to be the reality of the Holy of Holies. This means that the Son is in the Father, that the Father is in the Son, and that the Son as the Spirit is the reality of the Holy of Holies. This implies and corresponds to the four *in*s in John 14:16-20. Verse 20 says, "In that day you will know that I am in My Father, and you in Me, and I in you," and verse 17 says, "The Spirit of reality ...shall be in you." The Son is in the Father, we are in the Son, the Son is in us, and we are indwelt by the Spirit of reality. This is the incorporation of the processed God with the regenerated believers.

The way to be incorporated into the tabernacle is to eat the hidden manna. The more we eat Christ, the more we are incorporated into the Triune God as a universal incorporation. By eating the hidden manna we are incorporated into the tabernacle. The tabernacle in the Old Testament was a figure of the New Jerusalem, which is called the tabernacle of God. As the tabernacle of God the New Jerusalem is the universal incorporation. This universal incorporation is God's eternal goal....The way to be in the New Jerusalem is to eat Christ. The more we eat Christ, the more we are incorporated into this universal incorporation. (*The Issue of Christ Being Glorified by the Father with the Divine Glory*, pp. 30-31)

Further Reading: The Issue of Christ Being Glorified by the Father with the Divine Glory, chs. 4-5

Enlightenment and inspiration: _____

_____

_____

_____

Morning Nourishment

John
14:21, 23   He who has My commandments and keeps them, he is the one who loves Me; and he who loves Me will be loved by My Father, and I will love him and will manifest Myself to him....If anyone loves Me, he will keep My word, and My Father will love him, and We will come to him and make an abode with him.

1 John
2:27   And as for you, the anointing which you have received from Him abides in you, and you have no need that anyone teach you; but as His anointing teaches you concerning all things and is true and is not a lie, and even as it has taught you, abide in Him.

To have Christ abiding in us is to have the Son and the Father coming to us and making an abode with us (John 14:23). When we have the words of Christ, the Spirit of reality, and the very God abiding in us, we surely have the Son and the Father abiding in us. We have both the Son and the Father coming to us and making an abode with us. This abode is a mutual abode. He becomes our abode, and we become His abode.

In John 14:23 the Lord said, "If anyone loves Me...My Father will love him." When we love the Son, the Father will love us. Then the Son will follow His Father to love us (v. 21). The Father and the Son both will love us because we love the Son. This issues in our enjoyment of the Son's manifestation (vv. 21-22). Our enjoyment of the Son's manifestation depends upon our loving Him. This is altogether not a doctrine but an experience. The Divine Trinity is not for doctrine but altogether for our experience. When we love the Son, both the Father and the Son love us, and at the same time, the Son manifests Himself to us. We enjoy His appearing. In other words, we enjoy His presence. (*Living in and with the Divine Trinity*, pp. 102-103)

Today's Reading

John 15:1-8 concerns Christ as the vine and the believers as branches in the vine. However, the way for us to abide in the vine is not fully developed in the Gospel of John....In his first Epistle John continued to show the way to abide in Christ. According to 1 John 2:27, the way to abide in Christ is to take care of the anointing....The anointing mentioned in 1 John comes from the holy anointing oil described in Exodus 30:23-25, which was a compound ointment. This anointing oil typifies the Spirit of Jesus Christ. The anointing gives us the way to abide in the vine.

Many branches are attached to a vine. The branches are not only attached to the vine but also abiding in the vine. The life-juice within the vine flows into the branches. By this flow the branches abide in the vine. The abiding of the branches in the vine is an illustration of the fellowship mentioned in 1 John 1:7. Fellowship is abiding, and abiding is carried out by the anointing....The Gospel of John mentions the abiding (15:4-7). Then the first Epistle of John mentions the anointing, which is the way to abide.

The way to abide is by the anointing. All believers have the Spirit within them, and this Spirit is not silent, passive, or inactive. He is very active and aggressive and is constantly moving and working within us. The moving and working of the Holy Spirit within us is the anointing....God's salvation is not merely an objective matter, something outside of our being. God's salvation is subjective; it is a person within us. This person is God Himself as the life-giving Spirit within every believer. Every one of us has this moving person living in us. (*Crucial Principles for the Christian Life and the Church Life,* pp. 31-32)

Further Reading: A Living of Mutual Abiding with the Lord in Spirit, ch. 3; *Abiding in the Lord to Enjoy His Life,* chs. 1-3, 7; *The Mending Ministry of John,* ch. 8; *Crucial Principles for the Christian Life and the Church Life,* ch. 3; *The Mystery of Christ,* ch. 7; *The Experience of Life,* ch. 7; *Life-study of 1 John,* msg. 25; *The Experience of Christ,* ch. 23

Enlightenment and inspiration: _____

_____

_____

_____

Morning Nourishment

John **If you abide in Me and My words abide in you, ask**
15:7 **whatever you will, and it shall be done for you.**

As we abide in the Lord, we must allow His words to abide in
us (v. 7). The word translated "words" is rhema in Greek, meaning
the instant and present spoken word. To let the Lord's instant
words abide in us is quite demanding. The Son desires to spread
His abiding in us. As He abides in us, He is always speaking. This
speaking is the rhema, the instant word. He mainly speaks one
word to us—no. However, at times His speaking is a requirement
or a demand. How we need to love Him and keep His instant
words! When He speaks the instant rhema, we must listen to it
and keep it. If we do not keep this instant word, we shall immediately be cut off from the fellowship. But if we do keep it, we shall
absorb all of the riches of His fullness, of His life, and have an
overflow of life for fruitbearing. (*Life-study of John,* pp. 409-410)

Today's Reading

In order for the Lord to abide in us, it is necessary to let His
words abide in us. The only possible way for the Lord to be practical to us is by His words....If we want to allow the Lord to abide in
us, we must let His words abide in us....Praise the Lord that we
have something very substantial, available, and practical in our
hands. We have the Word. We can read the Word and receive it
with our heart and our spirit. We can contact the word of the Lord
in our spirit day by day and even moment by moment. As long as
we are contacting the Lord's word, we are contacting the Lord
Himself.

Logos is the outward word as a message spoken or written; rhema
is the present, inward word. We have logos in our hands, but we
have rhema in our spirit. Logos is the written word as the expression of the living Christ; rhema is the word spoken within us by
the Spirit of Christ just at the time we need it. For example, perhaps while you are fellowshipping with another brother something
within tells you to stop talking. This is rhema. Perhaps you are
thinking about a certain matter that you want to do today, but again

something within you tells you not to do it. This also is rhema. We should not vaguely say that we abide in Christ and that Christ abides in us. We must be more precise and realize that we must deal with two kinds of words—the outward word and the inward word, the word in the Scriptures that is outside of us and the word in the spirit that is within us....We must deal with the written word without and the living word within, because by the written word without we have the explanation, definition, and expression of the mysterious Lord and by the living word within we have the experience of the abiding Christ and the presence of the practical Lord.

The inner rhema always corresponds with the outer logos. The Spirit speaking the rhema within never speaks differently from the written logos. The outer logos and the inner rhema always correspond with each other, and many times the inner rhema interprets the outer logos. Perhaps you read the written logos this morning but failed to understand it or to apply it to you in a living way. While you are working, the Spirit anoints you from within with the word, giving you the right meaning and even the right emphasis. You sense the living rhema with its living emphasis by the Spirit. As a result, you not only understand it in your mind but also apprehend it in your spirit. Now the outward, written word becomes the living word within your spirit. You can experience it and apply it in your life. In this way the logos becomes the rhema; the outer word becomes the inner word. We need to attend to the living rhema within, allowing it to have its full way within us. In order to allow the living word to have its free way within us, we must go along with it. In other words, we must be very submissive and obedient to the living rhema that is speaking now within us. Concentrating on the inner rhema will make the living Lord so real to us in our spirit. It will make Christ so available and practical. We shall sense the moving and the working of the Lord who energizes us inwardly. (*Life-study of John*, pp. 411-413)

Further Reading: Life-study of John, msgs. 32, 34

Enlightenment and inspiration: _____

_____

_____

_____

Hymns, #1163

1 He's the vine and we're the branches,
  We should e'er abide in Him,
  And let Him abide within us
  As the flow of life within.

    In the vine, in the vine,
    In the vine, in the vine,
    We would know Thee, Lord, more deeply,
    E'er abiding in the vine.

2 As we hear His instant speaking,
  He's the rich indwelling Word;
  To abide we must be faithful
  To the speaking that we've heard.

3 For 'tis here we know abiding
  In the real and deepest way;
  If we love our Lord completely,
  We would do whate'er He'd say.

4 Then His love abides within us,
  And in love abiding, we
  Know the joy of life-communion,
  Full and perfect harmony.

5 Oh, how precious this abiding,
  Oh, how intimate and sweet;
  As the fruit of life is added,
  And our joy is made complete.

Composition for prophecy with main point and sub-points: _____

The Practice of the Divine Righteousness

Scripture Reading: 1 John 2:28—3:10a

Day 1
I. **The fellowship of the divine life and the teaching of the divine anointing should have an issue—the expression of the righteous God (1 John 2:29; 3:7).**

II. **The word *righteous* in 2:29 refers to the righteous God in 1:9 and to Jesus Christ the Righteous in 2:1:**

A. The righteousness of God is what God is in His actions with respect to justice and righteousness (Rom. 1:17; 3:21-22; 10:3):

1. Righteousness is related to God's actions and activities (Rev. 16:7; 19:2).

2. God is righteous in His ways—His governing principles by which He does things; righteousness is the nature of God's acts (15:3; Psa. 103:7).

3. God is righteous in the blood of Jesus His Son, which has fulfilled God's righteous requirements so that He may forgive us our sins (1 John 1:9).

B. In ascension Jesus Christ is the Righteous (2:1):

1. As the ascended One in the heavens, Christ is working and ministering righteously.

2. As our Representative, or Attorney, in the heavenly court, Christ is the righteous One (v. 1).

Day 2
III. **There are two aspects of Christ being righteousness from God to the believers (1 Cor. 1:30; Matt. 5:20):**

A. The first aspect is that Christ is the believers' righteousness for them to be justified before God objectively at the time of their repenting unto God and believing into Christ (Rom. 3:24-26; Acts 13:39; Gal. 3:24b, 27).

B. The second aspect is that Christ is the believers'

righteousness lived out of them as the manifestation of God, who is the righteousness in Christ given to the believers for them to be justified by God subjectively (Rom. 4:25; 1 Pet. 2:24a; James 2:24; Matt. 5:20; Rev. 19:8).

Day 3 IV. **To practice the divine righteousness is to do righteousness habitually, continually, and unintentionally as a way of life in our daily living (1 John 2:29; 3:7):**

A. With the divine birth as the basis and the divine life as the means, we can live a life that practices the divine righteousness (2:25, 29; 3:9).

B. The practice of the divine righteousness is a spontaneous living that issues from the divine life within us, with which we have been begotten of the righteous God (1:1-2; 2:29; 5:1).

C. The practice of the divine righteousness is a living expression of God, who is righteous in all His deeds and acts (Rev. 15:3).

D. The practice of the divine righteousness is not merely outward behavior but the manifestation of the inward life; it is not merely an act of purpose but the flow of life from within the divine nature, of which we partake (2 Pet. 1:4; Rev. 22:1-2):

1. We have a righteous nature within us, a nature that is of our new man (Eph. 4:24; Col. 3:10).

2. As we obey the inner anointing, the moving of the Triune God within us, we will live habitually according to this righteous nature (1 John 2:27).

Day 4 E. As the result of being saturated with the Triune God, we become His expression; in particular, because God is righteous, when we express Him, we express His righteousness (3:7).

F. Because we abide in the righteous God and He is saturating us with what He is, we express His righteousness by living a righteous life habitually and unintentionally (2:29).

G. To practice the divine righteousness—to live a righteous life that is the expression of the righteous God—is to purify ourselves (3:3):

1. *Righteous* in verse 7 equals *pure* in verse 3.

2. To be righteous is to be pure, without any stain of sin, lawlessness, and unrighteousness, even as Christ is.

H. To practice sin (lawlessness) is to live a life which is not under the ruling principle of God over man; to practice righteousness is to live rightly under the principle of God's ruling (vv. 4, 7).

Day 5   V. **To practice the divine righteousness is to live out and express the righteousness of God in a full and complete way (Matt. 5:20; Rom. 8:4; 2 Cor. 3:9; 5:21; Phil. 3:9; Psa. 89:14; Rev. 19:7-8; 2 Pet. 3:13):**

A. To practice the divine righteousness is to live a life that is right with God, persons, things, and matters before God according to His righteous and strict requirements (Matt. 5:20).

B. To practice the divine righteousness is to live out the subjective righteousness of God, which is actually God Himself in Christ lived out through us to become a daily living that is right with God and man (Phil. 3:9).

C. To practice the divine righteousness is to live Christ; if we live Christ, we will be the most righteous persons, for the Christ who lives within us will make us right in everything and with everyone (1:20-21a).

D. To practice the divine righteousness is to have the righteousness that is the outward expression of the Christ who lives within us as the life-giving Spirit; as Christ lives in us as the life-giving Spirit and we live Him out, our living will express the divine righteousness (1 Cor. 15:45b; 6:17; 2 Cor. 3:6, 9, 17-18).

Day 6   E. To practice the divine righteousness is to express the image of God; the Spirit is the essence of God living, moving, and acting within us, and righteousness is the essence of God manifested outwardly as God's image (Eph. 4:24; Col. 3:10).

F. To practice the divine righteousness is to be right with God in our being; this is to have an inner being that is transparent and crystal clear, that is in the mind and will of God, and that is the righteousness of God (2 Cor. 5:21).

G. To practice the divine righteousness is to live in the reality of the kingdom of God and under the throne of God, which is established with righteousness as the foundation (Rom. 14:17; Psa. 89:14).

H. To practice the divine righteousness is to be clothed with righteousnesses to be the bride of Christ adorned with bright, shining righteousness (Rev. 19:7-8).

Morning Nourishment

Rom. 1:17 ...As it is written, "But the righteous shall have life and live by faith."

Rev. 16:7 ...Yes, Lord God the Almighty, true and righteous are Your judgments.

1 John 1:9 If we confess our sins, He is faithful and righteous to forgive us our sins and cleanse us from all unrighteousness.

2:1 ...If anyone sins, we have an Advocate with the Father, Jesus Christ the Righteous.

The word "righteous" in 1 John 2:29 refers to the righteous God in 1:9 and Jesus Christ the Righteous in 2:1. In this word to all the recipients, beginning from 2:28, the apostle turns his emphasis from the fellowship of the divine life in 1:3—2:11 and the anointing of the Divine Trinity in 2:12-27 to the righteousness of God. The fellowship of the divine life and the anointing of the Divine Trinity should have an issue, that is, should issue in the expression of the righteous God. (*Life-study of 1 John,* p. 213)

Today's Reading

What is the righteousness of God? The righteousness of God is what God is in His action with respect to justice and righteousness. God is just and right. Whatever God is in His justice and righteousness constitutes His righteousness.

Revelation 15:3 says, "Great and wonderful are Your works, Lord God the Almighty! Righteous and true are Your ways, O King of the nations!" God's works are His acts, whereas God's ways are His governing principles. God's ways are righteous in His principles. If you know God's ways, you will not need to wait to see His works in order to praise Him. Although His works have not yet come, you will know they will come because you know the governing principles by which God does things. God's ways are righteous according to His principles.

First John 1:9 says, "If we confess our sins, He is faithful and righteous to forgive our sins and cleanse us from all unrighteousness." God is faithful in His word (1:10) and righteous in the blood of Jesus His Son (1:7). His word is the word of the truth of His gospel (Eph. 1:13), which tells us that He will forgive us our sins because of Christ (Acts 10:43), and the blood of Christ has fulfilled His righteous requirements that He may forgive us our sins (Matt. 26:28). If we confess our sins, He, according to His word and based on the redemption through the blood of Jesus, forgives us, because He must be faithful in His word and righteous in the blood of Jesus. Otherwise, God would be unfaithful and unrighteous.

In ascension Christ is the Righteous [1 John 2:1b]....Our Lord Jesus is the only righteous man among all men. Only He is qualified to be our Advocate to care for us in our sinning condition and restore us to a righteous condition so that our Father, who is righteous, may be appeased.

Instead of saying "Jesus Christ the Righteous," we may say "Jesus Christ, the right One." Jesus Christ certainly is the One who is right, the right One, and only this right One can be our Advocate with the Father, taking care of our case.

Christ was the righteous One in His earthly life, for He was right with God and man. Now, in the heavens, He is still the righteous One. As the ascended One in the heavens, Christ does everything in a righteous way. He is working and ministering righteously. If He were not acting righteously in the heavens, He could not be in God's presence. Whatever Christ is doing now in the heavens to intercede for us and to minister life to us as the High Priest according to the order of Melchisedec, He does righteously. His heavenly ministry of life today is a ministry in righteousness. In ascension He truly is the Righteous.

As our Representative, or Attorney, in the heavenly court, Christ is the righteous One. Just as an attorney cannot practice law if he is unrighteous, a lawbreaker, so Christ could not be our Attorney if He were not righteous. Christ, the Righteous, is surely the Lawkeeper, thus qualified to be our Advocate, our Attorney. (*The Conclusion of the New Testament,* pp. 87-88, 343)

Further Reading: The Conclusion of the New Testament, msgs. 9, 31

Enlightenment and inspiration: _____
_____
_____
_____

Morning Nourishment

Matt. ...Unless your righteousness surpasses that of the
5:20 scribes and Pharisees, you shall by no means enter
into the kingdom of the heavens.

1 Cor. But of Him you are in Christ Jesus, who became
1:30 wisdom to us from God: both righteousness and
sanctification and redemption.

Acts And from all the things from which you were not
13:39 able to be justified by the law of Moses, in this One
everyone who believes is justified.

Rev. And it was given to her that she should be clothed
19:8 in fine linen, bright *and* clean; for the fine linen is
the righteousnesses of the saints.

There are two aspects of Christ being righteousness from God
to the believers. The first aspect is that He is the believers' righteousness for them to be justified before God objectively at the time
of their repenting unto God and believing into Christ (Rom. 3:24-
26; Acts 13:39; Gal. 3:24b, 27)....Christ is our beauty given by God
to us to be put on us as our clothing....This is outward, objective.

The second aspect is that Christ is the believers' righteousness
lived out of them as the manifestation of God, who is the righteousness in Christ given to the believers for them to be justified by God
subjectively (Rom. 4:25; 1 Pet. 2:24a; James 2:24; Matt. 5:20; Rev.
19:8). (*Crystallization-study of the Epistle to the Romans*, pp. 53-54)

Today's Reading

We can see the two aspects [of Christ as our righteousness]—
outward and inward. Christ is put on us, and Christ enters into us
to live God out of us to be our subjective righteousness.

These two aspects are typified by the best robe and the fattened
calf in Luke 15:22-23. The best robe typifies Christ as God's righteousness given to the believers to cover them outwardly before God
as their objective righteousness. The fattened calf typifies Christ as
God's righteousness given to the believers as their life supply for
them to live out God in Christ as their subjective righteousness.

In Luke 15 when the prodigal son came back to the father, the father told his slaves to bring out the best robe and put it on his son. This robe replaced the rags (Isa. 64:6) of the returned prodigal. Surely the rags would not be pleasant to the father. But the father told the slaves to take the best robe and put it on his son as a new dress to cover him. Thus, he became a new man, but just outwardly.

Immediately following this, the father said, "And bring the fattened calf; slaughter it, and let us eat and be merry" (Luke 15:23). Even though the robe was put upon the prodigal son, he was still hungry. He could have said, "Father, I need something to eat. I was eating the pigs' food. I am starved to death. Father, I don't need this robe; I need something to eat." But the father could say, "Son, if you are so poor, in rags, I cannot serve you anything. I must beautify you first by dressing you up. Then you match me. Then I can serve you with a pleasant meal, the fattened calf."

The best robe is a type of Christ being righteousness to us outwardly. The fattened calf typifies the subjective Christ entering into us to be enjoyed, digested, and assimilated by us to become our tissue, to become us. By eating the fattened calf, the prodigal son's face would be transformed. He came back with a pale face. But after eating the fattened calf, his face would become shining, bright and colorful. This is Christ given by God to us as righteousness in two aspects: as the outward righteousness to beautify us and as the inward righteousness to supply us to live Himself out of us to be God's pleasure.

These two aspects of Christ as righteousness are also typified by the two garments of the queen in Psalm 45:13-14. Solomon had a queen, and that queen had two garments. The first one corresponds with the objective righteousness, which is for our justification. The other garment corresponds with the subjective righteousnesses (Rev. 19:8), which are for our victory. This garment is equivalent to the wedding garment in Matthew 22:11-12. (*Crystallization-study of the Epistle to the Romans,* pp. 54-55)

Further Reading: Crystallization-study of the Epistle to the Romans, msgs. 5-6

Enlightenment and inspiration: _____

_____

_____

_____

Morning Nourishment

1 John   If you know that He is righteous, you know that every-
2:29   one who practices righteousness also has been begotten of Him.
3:7   Little children, let no one lead you astray; he who
practices righteousness is righteous, even as He is
righteous.
Rev.   And they sing the song of Moses, the slave of God, and
15:3   the song of the Lamb, saying, Great and wonderful
are Your works, Lord God the Almighty! Righteous
and true are Your ways, O King of the nations!
Eph.   And put on the new man, which was created accord-
4:24   ing to God in righteousness and holiness of the reality.

According to John's word in 1 John 2:29, if we know that God is
righteous, we "know that everyone who practices righteousness
also has been begotten of Him." To practice righteousness is not
merely to do righteousness occasionally and purposely as some
particular act; it is to do righteousness habitually and unintentionally as one's common daily living. It is the same in 3:7. This is
an automatic living that issues from the divine life within us, with
which we have been begotten of the righteous God. Hence, it is a
living expression of God, who is righteous in all His deeds and acts.
It is not merely outward behavior, but the manifestation of the
inward life; not merely an act of purpose, but the flow of life from
within the divine nature we partake of. This is the first condition
of the life that abides in the Lord. It is all due to the divine birth,
which is indicated by the word "has been begotten of Him" and
the title "children of God" in 3:1. (*Life-study of 1 John,* pp. 213-214)

Today's Reading

John's writings on the mysteries of the eternal divine life place
much emphasis on the divine birth (1 John 3:9; 4:7; 5:1, 4, 18; John
1:12-13), which is our regeneration (3:3, 5). It is the greatest wonder in the entire universe that human beings could be begotten of
God, and sinners could be made children of God! Through such an
amazing divine birth we have received the divine life, which is the

eternal life (1 John 1:2), as the divine seed sown into our being (3:9). Out of this seed all the riches of the divine life grow from within us. It is by this that we abide in the Triune God and live the divine life in our human living, a life that does not practice sin (3:9), but practices righteousness (2:29), loves the brothers (5:1), overcomes the world (5:4), and is not touched by the evil one (5:18).

We Christians, as children of God, should be saturated with the righteous God so that spontaneously we live a life that practices righteousness habitually and unintentionally. Instead of doing a particular act of righteousness for a certain purpose, we practice righteousness as our common daily life. This is an issue of the fellowship of the divine life and the anointing of the Divine Trinity. Furthermore, this is an expression of the righteous God. Through abiding in the righteous God, we are infused and saturated with Him. Then our living becomes an expression of the righteous God with whom we have been infused and saturated. This righteous God then becomes our righteous living, our daily righteousness. This practice of righteousness is not merely outward behavior, but the manifestation of the inward life....This is not an act done for a purpose; it is the flow of life from within the divine nature of which we partake.

The anointing is the moving of the Triune God within us. This means that our God has become subjective to us. The Triune God—the Father, the Son, and the Spirit—is within our spirit. Day by day this processed Triune God as the anointing leads us into the virtues of the divine life, the virtues we have received through the divine birth. These virtues include living a righteous life, loving the brothers, and overcoming all negative things. To live a righteous life is to have a life that is right with God and with man. Righteousness is a matter of being right with both God and man. Therefore, to practice righteousness is to have a life that is right with God and man. (*Life-study of 1 John*, pp. 214, 224, 232)

Further Reading: Life-study of 1 John, msg. 25; Life-study of Revelation, msg. 54

Enlightenment and inspiration: _____

_____

_____

Morning Nourishment

1 John And everyone who has this hope *set* on Him purifies
3:3-4 himself, even as He is pure. Everyone who practices
       sin practices lawlessness also, and sin is lawlessness.
   6   Everyone who abides in Him does not sin; everyone
       who sins has not seen Him or known Him.
   9   Everyone who has been begotten of God does not
       practice sin, because His seed abides in him; and he
       cannot sin, because he has been begotten of God.

As the result of being saturated with the Triune God, we
become His expression. Because we have been saturated with
Him, we express Him. In a sense, after the cloth has been saturated with the paint, it becomes the paint and expresses not itself
but the paint with which it has been saturated. Likewise, as the
result of being thoroughly saturated with the Triune God, we
shall express Him. In particular, because God is righteous, when
we express Him, we shall express His righteousness. (*Life-study
of 1 John*, p. 219)

Today's Reading

In 1 John 2:29 John speaks not merely of doing righteousness but of practicing righteousness, that is, of doing righteousness continually and habitually as a way of life. A dog, for
example, habitually, continually, and unintentionally stands on
four legs. For a dog to try to stand upright on two legs and walk
like a man would not be a practice but an attempt to act like a
human being. Likewise, an unbeliever may do something righteous for a particular purpose. However, as children of God, we
practice righteousness spontaneously, habitually, automatically,
continually, and without a purpose. This means that we do not
purposely intend to do righteousness; rather, we practice righteousness because this is the living of the divine life that is within
us. Because we abide in the righteous God and He is saturating
us with what He is, we express His righteousness by living a
righteous life unintentionally and habitually.

Because He is righteous, we shall continually express the

divine righteousness by practicing righteousness habitually and unintentionally. This is to practice the divine righteousness by virtue of the divine birth.

The hope spoken of in 3:3 is the hope of being like the Lord, the hope of bearing the likeness of the Triune God. Our expectation is that we shall be like Him….Because we have this hope, we purify ourselves. According to the context of this section, from 2:28 through 3:24, to purify ourselves is to practice righteousness (3:7; 2:29), to live a righteous life that is the expression of the righteous God (1:9), the righteous One (2:1). This is to be pure without any stain of unrighteousness, even as that One is perfectly pure. This also describes the life that abides in the Lord.

To practice sin [in 3:4] is not merely to commit sin as occasional acts, but to live in sin (Rom. 6:2), to live a life which is not under the ruling principle of God over man.

No one who is a child of God practices sin habitually. We may sin occasionally, but we do not practice sin habitually….Instead of practicing sin, those who are children of God practice righteousness habitually.

In verse 7 John says, "Little children, let no one lead you astray; he who practices righteousness is righteous, even as He is righteous." To practice righteousness is to live a righteous life, living uprightly under God's ruling principle. This, according to the following verse, means not to practice sin, and, according to verse 4, not to practice lawlessness.

According to the context, "righteous" here equals "pure" in verse 3. To be righteous is to be pure, without any stain of sin, lawlessness, and unrighteousness, even as Christ is pure. The emphasis of the apostle John is that as long as we are children of God having the divine life and the divine nature, we certainly will habitually live a life of righteousness. (*Life-study of 1 John*, pp. 219-220, 226-228)

Further Reading: Life-study of 1 John, msg. 26; Life-study of Philippians, msg. 51

Enlightenment and inspiration: _____

_____

_____

Morning Nourishment

Phil. 3:9 And be found in Him, not having my own righteousness which is out of the law, but that which is through faith in Christ, the righteousness which is out of God *and* based on faith.

2 Cor. 5:21 Him who did not know sin He made sin on our behalf that we might become the righteousness of God in Him.

2 Pet. 3:13 But according to His promise we are expecting new heavens and a new earth, in which righteousness dwells.

In Philippians 3:9 Paul does not speak merely in a general way, but in a very definite way...."Not having my own righteousness...but...the righteousness which is out of God" is the condition in which Paul desired to be found in Christ. He wanted to live not in his own righteousness, but in the righteousness of God, and to be found in such a transcendent condition, expressing God by living Christ, not by keeping the law.

Before Paul was saved, he had no idea that Christ could be his righteousness. The righteousness of the law is the righteousness which comes from man's own effort to keep the law, as mentioned in verse 6. Formerly, Paul lived in that righteousness which was according to the law. Others could invariably find him enveloped by the righteousness of the law. But now Paul's desire was to be observed as a person living in Christ and having Christ as his righteousness. (*Life-study of Philippians,* p. 164)

Today's Reading

The expression "faith in Christ" [in Philippians 3:9] implies our believing in Christ. Such faith issues from our knowing and appreciating Christ. It is Christ Himself infused into us through our appreciation of Him, who becomes our faith in Him. Hence, it is also the faith in Christ that brings us into an organic union with Him.

The righteousness which is out of God and based on faith is that righteousness which is God Himself lived out of us to be our righteousness through our faith in Christ. Such righteousness is

the expression of God, who lives in us. It is based on faith because
...faith is the basis, the condition, for us to receive and possess the
righteousness out from God, the highest righteousness, which is
Christ (1 Cor. 1:30). (*Life-study of Philippians,* pp. 164-165)

God's intention is that we express Him with His image. However, if we would express God in this way, we need to have His life.
The life of God is signified by the tree of life in Genesis 2:9. The life
within is the Spirit, and the image outwardly for expression is
righteousness. Praise the Lord for the new covenant ministry with
the two aspects of life and expression! Inwardly we have the Spirit
as life, and outwardly we have righteousness as our expression.

Among all the people on earth, the most righteous persons are
those who live Christ. Whenever you live Christ, you will be right
in every way. You will not need anyone to teach you to be right, for
the Christ who lives within you will make you right in everything
and right with everyone. If we are careless with our things or in
the way we close a door, this is an indication that we are not living
Christ. If we truly live Christ, we shall close a door in a right
way....If the Bible contained a rule for every aspect of our daily
living, it would be too big for any of us to carry. It is the Spirit
within us who makes us righteous in our living. What we need is
more inscribing of the Spirit. The ministry of the new covenant is
a ministry of the Spirit.

When we are inscribed with the Spirit, the divine essence is
imparted into our being. This essence causes the process of spiritual metabolism to take place within us. As a result of this process, we are transformed into the Lord's image.

We have seen that to be transformed into the Lord's image
from glory to glory is to be transformed from the Spirit to the
Spirit. If we experience such an inward transformation, spontaneously we shall have righteousness as our outward appearance.
Then we shall be right with God, with others, and with ourselves.
(*Life-study of 2 Corinthians,* pp. 222-223)

Further Reading: Life-study of 2 Corinthians, msgs. 25-26

Enlightenment and inspiration: _____

_____

_____

_____

Morning Nourishment

Rom. For the kingdom of God is not eating and drinking,
14:17 but righteousness and peace and joy in the Holy Spirit.
Psa. Righteousness and justice are the foundation of Your
89:14 throne;/Lovingkindness and truth go before Your face.
Heb. But of the Son, "Your throne, O God, is forever and ever,
1:8-9 and the scepter of uprightness is the scepter of Your
kingdom. You have loved righteousness and hated
lawlessness; therefore God, Your God, has anointed
You with the oil of exultant joy above Your partners."

The Spirit and righteousness are both related to our expressing the image of God...[because] the Spirit and righteousness are actually God Himself. God as the Spirit is moving in you as a substance and living in you as an essence, for He Himself has been added into your being by the new covenant ministry. Thus, inwardly you have the Spirit. The righteousness you express outwardly is also God Himself. Therefore, you are not only right in so many ways, and you are not only righteous, but you have God Himself as your righteousness. God as righteousness becomes your appearance, your expression....This is the essence of the new covenant ministry. (*Life-study of 2 Corinthians*, pp. 221-222)

Today's Reading

If you are infused and saturated by the life-giving Spirit, your inner being will become transparent. Then you will know what is in the Lord's mind. You will also understand what the will of the Lord is. Spontaneously, you will be in His will and do His will. As a result, you become right with Him. Moreover, you will realize how you should act toward others and even how you should deal with your material possessions. Then you will become a righteous person, one who is right in small things as well as in great things, one who is right with God, with others, and with himself. This is a person who expresses God, for his righteousness is the image of God, God expressed.

Paul's word in Romans 14:17 corresponds to what is written in the Old Testament. According to Psalm 89:14, righteousness is the foundation of God's throne. This verse can also be translated to say that righteousness is the establishment of God's throne. God's throne is established with righteousness as the foundation....Where God's righteousness is, there His kingdom is also.

Righteousness first issues in the image of God. Then righteousness establishes the kingdom of God. In Romans 8 we have righteousness and God's image, and in Romans 14 we have righteousness and God's kingdom. Both the image and the kingdom are based on righteousness.

The goal of the new covenant ministry is to minister the all-inclusive Spirit of the processed Triune God into others to be their supply. Simultaneously, this ministry dispenses Christ into the believers as their righteousness. Then as the believers live and walk according to the Spirit, they will be in a condition that expresses God and that gives an impression of the Son of God. Furthermore, they will actually be the kingdom of God established in righteousness, set in order, and properly headed up. They will also have peace and joy in the Holy Spirit.

The bride [in Revelation 19:7 and 8] refers to redeemed and transformed tripartite mankind. This bride will wear white linen, which is the righteousnesses of the saints.

If we would have a share in this bride, who is adorned with bright, shining, pure righteousness, we need to adorn ourselves with righteousness. Day by day we need to prepare bright linen clothing to cover ourselves. This is our daily righteousness.

How can we produce such a garment of righteousness? We produce it by walking daily according to the Spirit of life and by having a life that is a life of the Spirit. If we prepare our wedding garment day by day, month by month, and year by year by living such a life in the Spirit, we shall not be found naked when the Lord comes. Instead, at His coming, we shall be wearing a bright, pure wedding garment. (*Life-study of 2 Corinthians,* pp. 242-243, 258-260)

Further Reading: Life-study of 2 Corinthians, msgs. 27-29

Enlightenment and inspiration: _____

_____

_____

_____

Hymns, #1099

1   The queen in gold of Ophir
    At Thy right hand doth stand;
  King's daughters are the women
    Who fill Thy honored band.
  The church in all her glory
    Shall match her glorious King,
  And all the saints, the women,
    Thy likeness there shall bring.

2   O daughter, now consider,
    E'en now incline thine ear:
  Remember not thy people
    And all thine own things here.
  Thy beauty then shall blossom—
    'Twill be the King's desire;
  For He thy worthy Lord is,
    Thy worship to inspire.

3   The daughter's glorious garments
    Are made of inwrought gold—
  Within the inner palace,
    How wondrous to behold!
  The glory of God's nature
    Is given her to wear,
  That all His holy being
    She may in life declare.

4   In clothing too embroidered
    She'll to the King be led,
  In that fine linen garment
    To be exhibited.
  'Tis by the Spirit's stitching
    That Christ in us is wrought,
  And with this glorious garment
    We'll to the King be brought.

5   What gladness and rejoicing
    When we the King shall see!
  We'll shout His worthy praises
    Through all eternity.
  And though the King we worship
    Or glory in the Queen,
  In all this blest enjoyment
    The glory goes to Him.

Composition for prophecy with main point and sub-points: _____

The Practice of the Divine Love

Scripture Reading: 1 John 2:3-11; 3:14-18; 4:7-12, 16-19;
2 John 5-6

Day 1
&
Day 2

I. **The love of God is God Himself; love is the inward essence of God and the heart of God (1 John 4:8, 16):**

A. God's predestination of us unto the divine sonship was motivated by the divine love (Eph. 1:4-5).

B. God's giving of His only begotten Son to us so that we may be saved from perdition judicially through His death and have the eternal life organically in His resurrection was motivated by the divine love (John 3:16; 1 John 4:9-10):

1. In the love of God, the Son of God saves us not only from our sins by His blood but also from our death by His life (Eph. 1:7; Rev. 1:5; Rom. 5:10).

2. God loved us and sent His Son as a propitiation for our sins in His judicial redemption with the intention that we might have life and live through Him in His organic salvation (1 John 2:1-2; 4:9-10; John 6:57; 14:19; Gal. 2:20).

3. God's excelling love is seen in His becoming a propitiatory sacrifice for our sins and the propitiation place for us to meet and be infused with God; God as love meets with us and speaks to us in the propitiating, redeeming, and shining Christ so that we can be infused with Him as love, mercy, and grace for His effulgent and radiant glory (Rom. 3:24-25; Heb. 4:16; Exo. 25:17, 22).

C. "I drew them with cords of a man, / With bands of love" (Hosea 11:4):

1. The phrase *with cords of a man, with bands of love* indicates that God loves us with His divine love not on the level of divinity but on the level of humanity; God's love is divine, but

it reaches us in the cords of a man, that is, through Christ's humanity.

2. The cords through which God draws us include Christ's incarnation, human living, crucifixion, resurrection, and ascension; it is by all these steps of Christ in His humanity that God's love in His salvation reaches us (Rom. 5:8).

3. Apart from Christ, God's everlasting love, His unchanging, subduing love, could not be prevailing in relation to us; God's unchanging love is prevailing because it is a love in Christ, with Christ, by Christ, and for Christ (vv. 5, 8; 8:35-39).

Day 3 II. **The practice of the divine love is the outcome of our enjoyment of the Triune God as the all-inclusive Spirit, the One who is moving and working within us as the anointing in the fellowship of the divine life to saturate us with all that the Triune God is, with all that He has done, and with all that He has obtained and attained (1 John 1:3; 2:3-11, 27):**

A. If we would experience and enjoy the divine love and have it become the love by which we love others, we need to know God experientially by continuously living in the divine life (vv. 3-6; Phil. 3:10a).

B. God first loved us in that He infused us with His love and generated within us the love with which we love Him and the brothers (1 John 4:19-21).

C. The life which we have received from God is a life of love; Christ lived in this world a life of God as love, and He is now our life so that we may live the same life of love in this world and be the same as He is (3:14; 5:1; 2:6; 4:17).

D. Our natural love must be put on the cross; one difference between God's love and our natural love is that it is very easy for our natural love to be offended.

E. We must be persons who are flooded with and

carried away by the love of Christ; the divine love should be like the rushing tide of great waters toward us, impelling us to live to Him beyond our own control (2 Cor. 5:14).

Day 4

F. The commandment regarding brotherly love is both old and new; old, because the believers have had it from the beginning of their Christian life; new, because in their Christian walk it dawns with new light and shines with new enlightenment and fresh power again and again (1 John 2:7-8; 3:11, 23; cf. John 13:34):

1. The commandments of the Lord are not merely injunctions; they are His words, which are spirit and life as a supply to us (6:63).

2. God's love is His inward essence, and the Lord's words supply us with His divine essence, with which we love Him and love the brothers.

3. We should love God and His children with the divine love that is conveyed to us through the words of the Lord to become our experience and enjoyment.

G. Our living in which we love one another in the love of God is the perfection and completion of this love in its manifestation in us (1 John 4:11-12; 2:5).

Day 5

III. **The church life is a life of brotherly love (4:7-8; 2 John 5-6; John 15:12, 17; Rev. 3:7; Eph. 5:2; cf. Jude 12a):**

A. The Body builds itself up in love (Eph. 4:16).

B. Our God-given, regenerated spirit is a spirit of love; we need a burning spirit of love to conquer the degradation of today's church (2 Tim. 1:7).

C. The one who loves God and the brothers is enjoying the divine life; the one who does not love is abiding in the satanic death (1 John 3:14; cf. 2 Cor. 11:2-3).

D. "Knowledge puffs up, but love builds up" (1 Cor. 8:1b; cf. 2 Cor. 3:6).

E. Loving one another is a sign that we belong to Christ (John 13:34-35).

F. Loving to be first in the church is versus loving all the brothers (3 John 9).

G. Just as the Lord Jesus laid down His soul-life so that we might have the divine life, we need to lose our soul-life and deny the self to love the brothers and minister life to them in the practice of the Body life (1 John 3:16; John 10:11, 17-18; 15:13; Eph. 4:29—5:2; 2 Cor. 12:15; Rom. 12:9-13).

H. We need to lose our soul-life by not loving the world with its pleasure; instead, taking in God and expressing God as love in the church life of brotherly love should be our joy, amusement, entertainment, and happiness (1 John 2:15-17; Matt. 16:25-26; Psa. 36:8-9; cf. 2 Tim. 3:4).

I. Brotherly love in the church life is expressed practically in our caring for the necessities of the needy saints without any self-serving purpose or outward self-display; in the sharing of material things with the needy saints, the grace of the Lord's life with His love flows among the members of the Body of Christ and is infused into them (1 John 3:17-18; Matt. 6:1-4; Rom. 12:13; 2 Cor. 8:1-7).

Day 6   IV. **First John 4 tells the secret of how to stand boldly before the judgment seat of Christ— abide in love (vv. 16-18; 2 Cor. 5:10, 14):**

A. To abide in love is to live a life in which we love others habitually with the love that is God Himself so that He may be expressed in us (1 John 4:16).

B. Perfect love is the love that has been perfected in us by our loving others with the love of God; such love casts out fear and has no fear of being punished by the Lord at His coming back (vv. 17-18; cf. Luke 12:46-47).

C. Love is the most excellent way for us to be anything or do anything for the building up of the church as the organic Body of Christ (1 Cor. 12:31b—13:8a).

Morning Nourishment

1 John **Beloved, let us love one another, because love is**
4:7-10 **of God, and everyone who loves has been begotten of**
God and knows God. He who does not love has not
known God, because God is love. In this the love of
God was manifested among us, that God sent His
only begotten Son into the world that we might have
life and live through Him. Herein is love, not that we
have loved God but that He loved us and sent His
Son as a propitiation for our sins.

Rom. **...The love of God has been poured out in our hearts**
5:5 **through the Holy Spirit, who has been given to us.**

God is love; we love because He first loved us (1 John 4:8, 19).
God does not want us to love with our natural love but with Him
as our love. God created man in His image (Gen. 1:26), which
means that He created man according to what He is. God's image
is what God is, and His attributes are what He is....God's first
attribute is love. God created man according to His attributes, the
first of which is love. Although created man does not have the
reality of love, there is something in his created being that wants
to love others. Even fallen man has the desire to love within him.
But that is just a human virtue, the very expression of the divine
attribute of love. When we were regenerated, God infused us with
Himself as love. We love Him because He first loved us. He initiated this love. (*The Vital Groups*, p. 69)

Today's Reading

God's predestination of us unto the divine sonship was motivated by the divine love. Ephesians 1:4-5 says that God chose us in
Christ before the foundation of the world "to be holy and without
blemish before Him in love, predestinating us unto sonship."...
God predestinated us unto sonship in love. John 3:16 says that God
so loved the world. He loved us before the foundation of the world.

God's giving of His only begotten Son to us that we may be
saved from perdition judicially through His death and have the

eternal life organically in His resurrection was motivated by the divine love (John 3:16; 1 John 4:9-10)....First John 4:10 says that God sent His Son to us as a propitiation for our sins. This is judicial through His death. Verse 9 says that God sent His Son to us that we may have life and live through Him. This is organic in His resurrection. John 3:16 should be read with 1 John 4:9-10. (*The Vital Groups*, pp. 69-70)

In the realm of grace the first thing we enjoy is the love of God. "The love of God has been poured out in our hearts through the Holy Spirit, who has been given to us" (Rom. 5:5). Many times in our Christian life we need encouragement and confirmation. As we pass through periods of suffering, we may have questions and doubts...about our circumstances. Although these doubts arise, we cannot deny that the love of God is within us. From the day we first called on the Lord Jesus, the love of God has been poured out into our hearts through the Holy Spirit. This means that the Spirit reveals, confirms, and assures us with the love of God.

Oh, the love of God has been poured into our hearts! Although we may be afflicted, poor, and depressed, we cannot deny the presence of God's love within us. Can we deny that Christ died for us? Christ died for ungodly sinners such as we. Once we were enemies, but Christ shed His blood on the cross to reconcile us to God. What love is this! If God has given us His own Son, surely He will not do anything to hurt us. God is sovereign. He knows what is best for us. The choice is His, not ours. Regardless of our preference, what God has planned for us will be our portion. Everything related to us has been prepared by our Father. We should simply pray, "Lord, have Your way. I simply want what You want. I leave everything entirely in Your hands." This is our response to God when we realize afresh that He loves us so and that His love has been poured into our hearts through the Holy Spirit. (*Life-study of Romans*, pp. 102-103)

Further Reading: The Vital Groups, msg. 8; *Life-study of Romans*, msg. 9; *Life-study of 1 John*, msg. 34

Enlightenment and inspiration: _____

_____

_____

_____

Morning Nourishment

Rom. Who shall separate us from the love of Christ? Shall
8:35-39 tribulation or anguish or persecution or famine or
nakedness or peril or sword? As it is written, "For Your
sake we are being put to death all day long; we have
been accounted as sheep for slaughter." But in all
these things we more than conquer through Him who
loved us. For I am persuaded that neither death nor
life nor angels nor principalities nor things present
nor things to come nor powers nor height nor depth nor
any other creature will be able to separate us from
the love of God, which is in Christ Jesus our Lord.

Although [Romans 8:35-36] certainly speaks of suffering, the
following verses [reveal that]…we are not defeated; we more than
conquer because God loves us [vv. 37-39]. Why does God care so
much for us and do so many things for us? Simply because we are
His beloved. No one can separate us from His love. Once He loves
us, He loves us forever with an eternal love. Nothing can separate us from Him. Because He loves us and because we are His
beloved, sooner or later we all shall be sanctified, transformed,
conformed, and glorified. (*Life-study of Romans,* p. 253)

Today's Reading

Paul was wise and very deep.…He composed three of the sections in Romans according to three of the attributes of God—His
righteousness, holiness, and glory. Eventually, however, Paul guides
us into the love of God.…Righteousness is the way of God, holiness is the nature of God, glory is the expression of God, and love
is the heart of God. After speaking of God's righteousness, holiness, and glory, Paul brings us into God's heart of love. Why has
God demonstrated His righteousness? Because man was fallen.
Man was wrong with God and needed His righteousness. Why
must God exercise His holiness? Because man is common. God
must sanctify all of His common, chosen ones. Why must God give
us His glory? Because all His chosen ones are low, mean, and vile.
Hence, He must exercise His glory to transfigure us. But what

was in God's heart originally? Love. Before God exercised His right-eousness, holiness, and glory, He loved us. Love was the fountain, love was the root, and love was the source of it all. God loved us before He predestinated us, He loved us before He called us, He loved us before He justified us, and He loved us before He glorified us. Before everything and anything else He loved us. Our salva-tion originated with the love of God. Love is the source of all that God does for us, and this love is His heart. Love was the source of God's eternal salvation which includes redemption, justification, reconciliation, sanctification, transformation, conformation, and glorification. Salvation began with God's heart of love.

Paul was persuaded that nothing can separate us from the love of God because he knew that this love does not derive from nor depend upon us, but upon God Himself. This love was not ini-tiated by us; it was initiated by God in eternity. Because of this Paul could say that we conquer in all things. Paul was convinced that nothing can "separate us from the love of God, which is in Christ Jesus our Lord."

This phrase "in Christ Jesus" is very significant. Why did Paul say this? Because he knew that there would be a problem if the love of God had been shown apart from Christ Jesus. Apart from Christ Jesus even a little sin such as losing our temper would sep-arate us from the love of God. However, the love of God is not merely the love of God in itself, but the love of God which is in Christ Jesus. Since the love of God is in Christ Jesus everything is insured, and we are assured that nothing can separate us from it. ...Paul was convinced that in all things "we more than conquer through Him who loved us." This does not mean that we in ourselves are able to overcome; it means that God is love and that Christ is Victor. God loves us and Christ has accomplished everything for us. Since God's love is eternal, His love in Christ Jesus is our security. We are not only under God's righteousness, holiness, and glory, but we are in His heart of love. (*Life-study of Romans,* pp. 253-255)

Further Reading: Life-study of Romans, msg. 21

Enlightenment and inspiration: _____

_____

_____

_____

Morning Nourishment

1 John **We know that we have passed out of death into life
3:14 because we love the brothers. He who does not
love abides in death.**

5:1 **Everyone who believes that Jesus is the Christ has
been begotten of God, and everyone who loves Him
who has begotten loves him also who has been
begotten of Him.**

The second condition [of the divine fellowship] is loving God
and the brothers. In order to fulfill this condition, we need to know
God...experientially by continuously living in the divine life. Our
daily life should be a life of knowing God constantly, for our life
should be a life of living God. As long as we live God, we shall constantly know Him.

If we would experience and enjoy the divine love and have it
become the love by which we love God and others, we need to
know God experientially. This is the basic requirement for having
the love of God become our love. (*Life-study of 1 John,* p. 149)

Today's Reading

When we know God, we keep the Lord's commandment. To
keep the Lord's commandment means that we take His word....
The Lord's word is not merely a command or injunction; it is also
a supply of life to us. The Lord's word always supplies life in our
spirit....Whenever we receive the Lord's word and put it into
practice, immediately we have the life supply within us.

The Lord's word is different from the Mosaic law. The Mosaic
law is an injunction with demands and requirements, but without any supply. However, whatever the Lord commands us in the
New Testament is a supplying word. His life supply backs up His
commandment. His commandment is not merely an injunction
requiring us to do something; it is also a word that always supplies whatever it demands. The Lord's word even supplies us with
the Lord Himself as life and as the Spirit. Therefore, we may
experience Him and enjoy Him. If we know Him, we shall keep
His word. By keeping His word we enjoy His supply.

When we keep the Lord's word and receive His supply, the love of God will be perfected within us. This means that as we receive the supply of the Lord's word, the love of God becomes our enjoyment, and this enjoyment issues in a love for God and the brothers.

If we would fulfill the second condition of the divine fellowship—the requirement that we love God and the brothers—we must know God. If we know Him, we shall keep His word. If we keep His word, we shall receive His supply of life. Then the love of God will be perfected in us. Our experience and enjoyment of God's love will issue in a love for God and the brothers. This is the fulfillment of the second requirement for maintaining the divine fellowship. (*Life-study of 1 John,* pp. 149-150)

First John 4:19 says, "We love because He first loved us." God first loved us in that He has infused us with His love and generated within us the love with which we love Him and love the brothers (v. 20). First John 4:20 says, "If anyone says, I love God, and hates his brother, he is a liar; for he who does not love his brother, whom he has seen, cannot love God, whom he has not seen."...We do not hate the brothers but love them habitually, living the divine life in the divine light and the divine love.

In 4:21 John says, "And this commandment we have from Him, that he who loves God love his brother also." The commandment here is the commandment of brotherly love (2:7-11; John 13:34). It is possible to summarize John's writing here in a simple way: God is love, and if we abide in Him, we shall love the brothers with Him as our love. This is John's basic thought in these verses.

In 4:17 John indicates that "as He is, so also are we in this world." As in 3:3 and 7, "He" refers to Christ. He lived in this world a life of God as love, and now He is our life so that we may live the same life of love in this world and be the same as He is now. As in 4:1, "world" [here] does not refer to the universe or the earth, but to human society on the earth, to the people, who are the components of the satanic world system. (*Life-study of 1 John,* pp. 312, 311)

Further Reading: Life-study of 1 John, msgs. 17, 34-35

Enlightenment and inspiration: _____

_____

_____

_____

Morning Nourishment

1 John
2:5

But whoever keeps His word, truly in this one the love of God has been perfected. In this we know that we are in Him.

7-8

Beloved, I am not writing a new commandment to you but an old commandment, which you have had from the beginning; the old commandment is the word which you heard. Yet again a new commandment I am writing to you, which is true in Him and in you because the darkness is passing away and the true light is already shining.

3:23

And this is His commandment, that we believe in the name of His Son Jesus Christ and love one another, even as He gave a commandment to us.

In 1 John 2:7 "the word" indicates the life supply. Whatever the Lord speaks is a word supplying us with life and spirit...Therefore, whenever we take the Lord's word and keep it, we receive the life supply.

In verse 8,...the commandment of brotherly love is both old and new....The relative pronoun "which"...should refer to the fact that the old commandment of brotherly love is new in the believers' Christian walk. This is true in the Lord, since He not only gave it to His believers, but also renews it in their daily walk all the time. This is true also in the believers, since they have not only received it once for all, but also are enlightened and refreshed by it repeatedly.

The old commandment and the new commandment are one. The reason for this is that the commandment is the word of the Lord, and the word of the Lord dawns as a new day dawns when the sun rises in the morning....The Lord's commandment, as His living word, shines as the dawning sun, and this shining swallows up darkness. (*Life-study of 1 John*, pp. 144-145)

Today's Reading

To take the Lord's word simply means to receive His divine supply. This supply is always contained in the Lord's word and is conveyed to us by His word. Therefore, the Lord's word is a channel through which the divine supply of life reaches us.

The word in [1 John 2:]5 is the totality, the aggregate, of all the commandments. No matter how many commandments there may be, as a whole these commandments are the word of the Lord. Hence, in verse 5 John speaks of keeping His word. By this he means keeping the word spoken either by the Lord Himself directly or spoken through the apostles.

In verse 5 John tells us that in the one who keeps the Lord's word, the love of God has been perfected.... "The love of God" here denotes our love toward God, which is generated by His love within us. The love of God, the word of the Lord, and God Himself are all related to one another. If we keep the Lord's word, God's love has been perfected in us. It is altogether a matter of the divine life, which is God Himself. God's love is His inward essence, and the Lord's word supplies us with this divine essence with which we love the brothers. Hence, when we keep the divine word, the divine love is perfected through the divine life by which we live.

The word "perfected" is very important....The love of God itself is perfect and complete in Himself. However, in us it needs to be perfected and completed in its manifestation. The love of God has been manifested to us in God's sending His Son to be both a propitiation and life to us (4:9-10). Yet, if we do not love one another with this love as it was manifested to us, that is, if we do not express it by loving one another with it as God expressed it to us, it is not perfectly and completely manifested. It is perfected and completed in its manifestation when we express it in our living by habitually loving one another with it. Our living in the love of God toward one another is its perfection and completion in its manifestation in us. Thus, others can behold God manifested in His love essence in our living in His love. (*Life-study of 1 John*, pp. 155, 131-132)

Further Reading: Life-study of 1 John, msgs. 15-16, 18, 27-28

Enlightenment and inspiration: _____

_____

_____

Morning Nourishment

2 John 5-6 And now I ask you, lady, not as writing a new commandment to you but that which we have had from the beginning, that we love one another. And this is love, that we walk according to His commandments. This is the commandment, even as you heard from the beginning, that you walk in love.

Love is the conclusion of all spiritual virtues and the factor of fruit-bearing that supplies us bountifully with the rich entrance into the kingdom of Christ (2 Pet. 1:5-11).

The Body of Christ builds itself up in love (Eph. 4:16). The phrase *in love* is used repeatedly in the book of Ephesians (1:4; 3:17; 4:2, 15-16; 5:2). God predestinated us unto sonship before the foundation of the world in love, and the Body of Christ builds itself up in love. The growth in life is in love. In the last few years we have appreciated the Lord's showing us the high peak of the divine revelation. My concern is that although we may talk about the truths of the high peak, love is absent among us. If this is the case, we are puffed up, not built up. The Body of Christ builds itself up in love.

First Corinthians 8:1b says, "Knowledge puffs up, but love builds up." Teaching without love may puff us up. We may listen to the messages of the ministry and become puffed up with mere knowledge. This does not build up. Love builds up. (*The Vital Groups*, pp. 72-73, 71)

Today's Reading

Paul said that we need to fan our gift into flame (2 Tim. 1:6). The main gift which God has given us is our regenerated human spirit with His Spirit, His life, and His nature. We must fan this gift into flame. This means that we have to stir up our spirit so that our spirit will be burning. Romans 12:11 says that we should be burning in spirit. If our spirit is not a spirit of love, our fanning it into flame will burn the whole recovery in a negative way. We must have a burning spirit of love, not a burning spirit of authority which damages. Whatever is mentioned in 2 Timothy is a requirement for us to face the degradation of the church. How can we overcome the degradation of the church? We must have a burning human spirit of love....Love prevails in this way.

First John 3:14b says that he who does not love abides in death. We may think that we are living, but we are dead because we do not love. If we do not love our brother, we abide in death and are dead, but if we do love him, we abide in life and are living.

First Corinthians 13 speaks of love, and then chapter fourteen begins by saying that we are to pursue love while we desire spiritual gifts (v. 1). Our desiring of gifts must go along with the pursuing of love. Otherwise, the gifts will puff us up.

To overcome the degradation of the church we need to pursue love with those who seek the Lord out of a pure heart (2 Tim. 2:22). We have to pursue love with a group of seekers of the Lord. This is a vital group.

The end of 1 Corinthians 12 reveals that love is the most excellent way (v. 31b)....Love is the most excellent way for us to prophesy and to teach others. Love is the most excellent way for us to be anything or do anything.

Love prevails. We should love everybody, even our enemies. If the co-workers and elders do not love the bad ones, eventually they will have nothing to do. We must be perfect as our Father is perfect (Matt. 5:48) by loving the evil ones and the good ones without any discrimination. We must be perfect as our Father because we are His sons, His species.

We should not consider that others are weak but we are not. This is not love. Love covers and builds up, so love is the most excellent way for us to be anything and to do anything for the building up of the Body of Christ. (*The Vital Groups*, pp. 73-75)

Further Reading: Messages for Building Up New Believers, vol. 3, ch. 47; The Speciality, Generality, and Practicality of the Church Life, ch. 7; An Autobiography of a Person in the Spirit, ch. 8; The Exercise of the Kingdom for the Building Up of the Church, ch. 6; The Spirit with Our Spirit, ch. 8

Enlightenment and inspiration: _____

_____

_____

_____

Morning Nourishment

1 John 4:16-18   **And we know and have believed the love which God has in us. God is love, and he who abides in love abides in God and God abides in him. In this has love been perfected with us, that we may have boldness in the day of the judgment because even as He is, *so* also are we in this world. There is no fear in love, but perfect love casts out fear because fear has punishment, and he who fears has not been perfected in love.**

[In 1 John 4:16] John says that we know and have believed the love which God has in us. This love is God's love in sending the Son to be our Savior (4:14)....This knowing involves experience and enjoyment....First we experience and enjoy, and then we believe....If we do not have much experience and enjoyment of God's love, we shall not be able to believe this love very much. But after we enjoy it and experience it, we surely believe the love which God has in us.

In 4:16 John says that he who abides in love abides in God and God abides in him. To abide in love is to live a life that loves others habitually with the love which is God Himself so that He may be expressed in us. To abide in God is to live a life which is God Himself as our inward content and outward expression so that we may be absolutely one with Him. God abides in us to be our life inwardly and our living outwardly. Thus, He may be one with us in a practical way. (*Life-study of 1 John*, pp. 309-310)

Today's Reading

In 1 John 4:17 John continues, "In this has love been perfected with us, that we may have boldness in the day of the judgment because even as He is, so also are we in this world." In our abiding in the love which is God Himself (v. 16) the love of God is perfected in us, that is, perfectly manifested in us, that we may have boldness without fear (v. 18) in the day of judgment.

In verse 17 John speaks of the love of God being perfected with us....The love of God itself is perfect and complete in Himself, but it still needs to be perfected in us. In order for God's love to be perfected in us, we need to experience this love. In our experience the love of God is perfected.

John says that if the love of God is perfected in us, we may have boldness in the day of judgment. The Greek word for "boldness" is *parresia,* meaning boldness of speech, confidence. In 3:21 boldness is for us to contact God in fellowship with Him. In 4:17 the boldness is for us to face the judgment at the judgment seat of Christ (2 Cor. 5:10) at His coming back (1 Cor. 3:13; 4:5; 2 Tim. 4:8). The judgment at the judgment seat of Christ will not be for eternal perdition or eternal salvation, but rather will be for reward or punishment. If we love the brothers with God as love, we shall have boldness in the day when Christ judges His believers at His judgment seat.

In verse 18 John goes on to say, "There is no fear in love, but perfect love casts out fear, because fear has punishment, and he who fears has not been perfected in love." A literal translation of the first part of this verse would be, "Fear is not in the love." "Fear" does not refer to the fear of offending God and being judged by Him (1 Pet. 1:17; Heb. 12:28), but to the fear that we *have* offended God and will be judged by Him. "Love" refers to the perfected love mentioned in the preceding verse, the love of God with which we love others. Perfect love is the love that has been perfected in us by our loving others with the love of God. Such love casts out fear and causes us to have no fear of being punished by the Lord at His coming back (Luke 12:46-47).

In 4:18 John tells us that he who fears has not been perfected in love. This means that the one who fears has not lived in the love of God so that it could be perfectly manifested in him.

First, John says in 4:12 and 17 that God's love needs to be perfected in us. Then in 4:18 he speaks of being perfected in love. This indicates that we and the divine love are mingled. When love is perfected in us, we are perfected in love, for we become the love, and the love becomes us. (*Life-study of 1 John,* pp. 310-312)

Further Reading: Life-study of 1 John, msgs. 29, 35

Enlightenment and inspiration: _____

_____

_____

_____

Hymns, #546

1   I love my Lord, but with no love of mine,
     For I have none to give;
  I love Thee, Lord, but all the love is Thine,
     For by Thy love I live.
  I am as nothing, and rejoice to be
  Emptied, and lost, and swallowed up in Thee.

2   Thou, Lord, alone, art all Thy children need,
     And there is none beside;
  From Thee the streams of blessedness proceed,
     In Thee the bless'd abide.
  Fountain of life, and all-abounding grace,
  Our source, our center, and our dwelling-place.

Hymns, #1159

1   Jesus Lord, I'm captured by Thy beauty,
     All my heart to Thee I open wide;
  Now set free from all religious duty,
     Only let me in Thyself abide.
  As I'm gazing here upon Thy glory,
     Fill my heart with radiancy divine;
  Saturate me, Lord, I now implore Thee,
     Mingle now Thy Spirit, Lord, with mine.

2   Shining One—how clear the sky above me!
     Son of Man, I see Thee on the throne!
  Holy One, the flames of God consume me,
     Till my being glows with Thee alone.
  Lord, when first I saw Thee in Thy splendor,
     All self-love and glory sank in shame;
  Now my heart its love and praises render,
     Tasting all the sweetness of Thy name.

3   Precious Lord, my flask of alabaster
     Gladly now I break in love for Thee;
  I anoint Thy head, Beloved Master;
     Lord, behold, I've saved the best for Thee.
  Dearest Lord, I waste myself upon Thee;
     Loving Thee, I'm deeply satisfied.
  Love outpoured from hidden depths within me,
     Costly oil, dear Lord, I would provide.

4   My Beloved, come on spices' mountain;
        How I yearn to see Thee face to face.
     Drink, dear Lord, from my heart's flowing fountain,
        Till I rest fore'er in Thine embrace.
     Not alone, O Lord, do I adore Thee,
        But with all the saints as Thy dear Bride;
     Quickly come, our love is waiting for Thee;
        Jesus Lord, Thou wilt be satisfied.

Composition for prophecy with main point and sub-points: _____

_____
_____
_____
_____
_____
_____
_____
_____
_____
_____
_____
_____
_____
_____
_____
_____
_____
_____
_____
_____
_____
_____
_____
_____
_____
_____
_____
_____
_____

The Testimony of God
and the Ministering of Life

Scripture Reading: 1 John 5:6-17

Day 1   **I. The testimony of God is the testimony by the water, the blood, and the Spirit that Jesus is the Son of God (1 John 5:6-10):**

A. In order to know the significance of the mystery of the water, the blood, and the Spirit, we need to understand the central thought of 1 John:

1. First John's central thought is that God in His Son as the Spirit has come into us as our life; this life brings us into a corporate fellowship with the Triune God and the believers, and this fellowship is the church life (1:1-7).

2. This central thought is focused on the Son of God (3:8; 4:9, 15; 5:5):

   a. The title *the Son of God* involves the imparting of the divine life (vv. 11-12).

   b. The Son of God was manifested for the purpose of imparting the divine life (4:9).

   c. By the water, the blood, and the Spirit, testimony was given as to His true identity—that He is the Son of God (5:5-9).

B. Jesus, the man of Nazareth, was attested to be the Son of God by the water He went through in His baptism (Matt. 3:16-17; John 1:31), by the blood He shed on the cross (19:31-35; Matt. 27:50-54), and also by the Spirit He gave not by measure (John 1:32-34; 3:34); by these three God has testified that Jesus is His Son given to us (1 John 5:7-10), that in Him we may receive His eternal life by believing into His name (vv. 11-13; John 3:16, 36; 20:31):

Day 2   1. The water refers to the baptism of the Lord Jesus (1 John 5:6, 8; Matt. 3:16-17):

   a. The first manifestation of Jesus as the

Son of God was His baptism by John (John
1:31-34).
  b. After He was baptized and came up from
     the death waters, the Spirit of God
     descended upon Him as a dove, and John
     testified that He was the Son of God
     (vv. 32, 34).
  c. A voice out of the heavens bore witness
     that this One was the beloved Son (Matt.
     3:17).
 2. The blood refers to the blood the Lord Jesus
    shed on the cross for our redemption (1 John
    5:6, 8):
  a. Some very special features were pres-
     ent at the crucifixion of Christ (Matt.
     27:51-53).
  b. The centurion and those with him guard-
     ing Jesus were frightened and said,
     "Truly this was the Son of God" (v. 54).
 3. The Spirit, who is the truth, the reality,
    testifies that Jesus is the Son of God, in
    whom is the eternal life; by thus testifying,
    He imparts the Son of God into us to be
    our life (1 John 5:6, 8; John 14:16-17; 15:26;
    Col. 3:4).
 4. Jesus was manifested as the Son of God
    in an open way by the water of baptism, by
    the blood He shed on the cross, and by the
    Spirit; by these three means God intro-
    duced His Son to mankind so that they
    might believe and have eternal life (John
    3:15-16; 20:31; 1 John 5:9-13).

Day 3 C. The water is for termination, the blood is for
         redemption, and the Spirit is for germination;
         we, the believers, have been terminated,
         redeemed, and germinated, and we are now in
         the proper church life, which is a life of termina-
         tion, redemption, and germination (Acts 2:38,
         42; 1 Cor. 2:2; 10:16-17).

D. The testimony of God is not only that Jesus is the Son of God but also that He gives to us eternal life, which is in His Son (1 John 5:10-13):

1. Because eternal life is in the Son, if we have the Son, we have eternal life (vv. 11-12).
2. God testified concerning His Son so that we might believe into His Son and have His divine life; if we believe into His Son, we receive and have His testimony in ourselves (v. 10).
3. The written words of the Scriptures are the assurance to the believers, who believe into the name of the Son of God, that they have eternal life (v. 13).

Day 4   II. In 1 John 5:14-17 there is the indication not only that we have eternal life and enjoy it but also that we can minister this life to other members of the Body:

A. Verses 14 through 17 show us that the eternal life within us can overcome death both in ourselves and in other members of the church.
B. Verse 16 is the only reference in the Bible to ministering life:
   1. To minister life is to impart life.
   2. When we have a surplus of life, we can minister from this supply to others (v. 16).

Day 5   C. Verse 14 speaks of prayer in the fellowship of eternal life:
   1. We should ask according to God's will, not according to our way, desire, or preference.
   2. The prayer that is according to God's will indicates that the praying one is abiding in the fellowship of the divine life and is also abiding in the Lord Himself, and thus he is truly one with the Lord (John 15:4-5).
   3. The knowing in 1 John 5:15 is based on the fact that after receiving the divine life we abide in the Lord and are one with Him in our praying to God in His name (John 15:7, 16; 16:23-24).

4. In 1 John 5:16 *he shall ask* and *he will give life* refer to the same person, that is, to the one who sees his brother sinning and asks concerning him:
   a. Such an asker, who is abiding in the Lord and who is one with the Lord (1 Cor. 6:17), becomes the means, the channel, by which God's life-giving Spirit can give life to the one for whom he is asking.
   b. This is a matter of the ministering of life in the fellowship of the divine life.
5. The vital point is that if we would pray for a brother according to what is described in 1 John 5:16, we need to be one with the Lord (John 15:7).

D. To be one who can give, impart, life to others, we must abide in the divine life and live, walk, and have our being in the divine life (1 John 1:1-7).

Day 6   E. What is described in 5:14-17 can be experienced only by those who are deep in the Lord:
1. We need to experience and enjoy the eternal life within us, and we need to minister this life by being a channel through which eternal life can flow to other members of the Body.
2. If we would be a channel for eternal life to flow out to others, we must be deep in the Lord, and we must know the Lord's heart by being in His heart (Psa. 25:14; Gen. 18:17, 22-33; Amos 3:7).

Morning Nourishment

1 John
5:6-9

This is He who came through water and blood, Jesus Christ; not in the water only, but in the water and in the blood; and the Spirit is He who testifies, because the Spirit is the reality. For there are three who testify, the Spirit and the water and the blood, and the three are unto the one thing. If we receive the testimony of men, the testimony of God is greater, because this is the testimony of God that He has testified concerning His Son.

The last mystery in the first Epistle of John is that of the water, the blood, and the Spirit. This Epistle is not a long one dealing with doctrinal points. John's way of writing is to touch only the main, crucial points....To know the real significance of this mystery, we must understand the central concept of this Epistle.

John's central thought is that God in His Son as the Spirit has come into us as our life. This life brings us into a fellowship—between Him and us and also with each other. This fellowship is corporate; there is the Father, the Son, and the Spirit, and there are the saints. This fellowship is actually the church life. The church life is a fellowship in the divine life. Since we have received God's life and nature as a seed of life within us, we have this wonderful person abiding in us as the Holy Spirit, a living, moving, active One. As such, He is the anointing to us. We abide in Him according to this anointing, and we let Him abide in us. By this abiding all things concerning the eternal purpose of God will be accomplished. (*The Seven Mysteries in the First Epistle of John,* pp. 67-68)

Today's Reading

This central concept [of 1 John] is focused on the Son of God. Whenever the New Testament uses this title, its significance always involves the imparting of the divine life. The Son of God was manifested for the purpose of imparting the divine life. "God gave to us eternal life and this life is in His Son. He who has the Son has the life...I have written these things to you that you may know that you have eternal life, to you who believe into the name of the Son of God" (1 John 5:11-13).

Why, then, is there the need of the witness of the water, the blood, and the Spirit? It is important for us to understand this in order that we may apply its value; otherwise, we are lacking in something. Yes, the Son of God came that we might have life. But He came in a way that puzzled people. He appeared as a Nazarene with no outward honor, with nothing to command respect. How could it be manifested that this One was in very fact the Son of God? It was by the water, the blood, and the Spirit that testimony was given as to His true identity. (*The Seven Mysteries in the First Epistle of John*, p. 68)

In 5:6...He, Jesus Christ, came as the Son of God so that we may be born of God and have the divine life (John 10:10; 20:31). It is in His Son that God gives us eternal life (1 John 5:11-13). Jesus, the Man of Nazareth, was testified to be the Son of God by the water He went through in His baptism (Matt. 3:16-17; John 1:31), by the blood He shed on the cross (John 19:31-35; Matt. 27:50-54), and also by the Spirit He gave not by measure (John 1:32-34; 3:34). By these three, God has testified that Jesus is His Son given to us (1 John 5:7-10) so that in Him we may receive His eternal life by believing in His name (5:11-13; John 3:16, 36; 20:31). The water of baptism terminates people of the old creation by burying them; the blood shed on the cross redeems those whom God has chosen from among the old creation; and the Spirit, who is the truth, the reality in life (Rom. 8:2), germinates those whom God has redeemed out of the old creation by regenerating them with the divine life. Thus they are born of God and become His children (John 3:5, 15; 1:12-13) to live a life that practices the truth (1 John 1:6), the will of God (2:17), the righteousness of God (2:29), and the love of God (3:10-11) for His expression. (*Life-study of 1 John*, pp. 321-322)

Further Reading: The Seven Mysteries in the First Epistle of John, ch. 8; *Life-study of 1 John*, msg. 36

Enlightenment and inspiration: _____

_____
_____
_____

Morning Nourishment

Matt. And having been baptized, Jesus went up immedi-
3:16-17 ately from the water, and behold, the heavens were
opened to Him, and He saw the Spirit of God descending like a dove and coming upon Him. And behold, a
voice out of the heavens, saying, This is My Son, the
Beloved, in whom I have found My delight.

27:54 Now the centurion and those with him guarding Jesus,
when they saw...the things that happened, became
greatly frightened, saying, Truly this was the Son of
God.

John But when the Comforter comes, whom I will send to
15:26 you from the Father, the Spirit of reality, who proceeds from the Father, He will testify concerning Me.

In 1 John 5:6 John says that the Spirit testifies because the
Spirit is the reality. The Spirit...testifies that Jesus is the Son of God,
in whom is the eternal life. By thus testifying, He imparts the Son
of God into us to be our life (Col. 3:4).

God testified that Jesus Christ is the Son of God [5:6-8]...in
three steps: by water, by the blood, and by the Spirit. The water
refers to the baptism of the Lord Jesus. According to the record of
the four Gospels, immediately after the Lord came up from the
water, the heavens were opened and a voice declared that He is
God's beloved Son. That was God's testimony that Jesus Christ is
His Son, the testimony by water, by baptism. Three and a half
years later, the Lord Jesus died on the cross, shedding His blood.
Someone standing near the cross testified, after the Lord died,
that He was God's Son. That was the testimony of God by blood
concerning Jesus Christ being the Son of God. Following this, we
have the testimony of the Spirit. In resurrection Christ became a
life-giving Spirit. (*Life-study of 1 John*, pp. 322-323)

Today's Reading

From John 1:31-34 we can see how the water bore witness to
Him. "In order that He might be manifested to Israel,...I came
baptizing in water. And John testified, saying, I beheld the Spirit

descending as a dove out of heaven, and He abode upon Him. And I did not know Him, but He who sent me to baptize in water, He said to me, He upon whom you see the Spirit descending and abiding upon Him, this is He who baptizes in the Holy Spirit. And I have seen and have testified that this is the Son of God." The first manifestation of Jesus as the Son of God was His baptism by John. This was the occasion when it was declared for the first time, "This is My Son, the Beloved, in whom I have found My delight" (Matt. 3:16-17)....In this scene the water and the Spirit were both present to introduce this little Jesus as nothing less than the Son of God.

How does the blood bear witness?

Some very special features were present at the crucifixion of Christ. For one thing, there was darkness over all the land (Matt. 27:45). For another, the Jews wanted to get the bodies off the cross before the upcoming great Sabbath (John 19:31). Thus they got permission for the soldiers to break the legs of the three who were being crucified in order to hasten their death. This the soldiers did to the two robbers. When they came to Jesus, however, they could see that He had already died. Instead of breaking His legs, one of the soldiers pierced His side with a spear; from that wound there came out blood and water.

These and the other things which happened caused fear in the heart of the centurion and those with him guarding Jesus, and they cried out, "Truly this was the Son of God" (Matt. 27:54). No doubt the centurion was thus saved. He believed that the crucified Nazarene was the Son of God.

Jesus, then, was manifested as the Son of God in an open way by the water of baptism, by the blood He shed on the cross, and by the Spirit. By these three means God introduced His Son to mankind that they might believe and have eternal life. (*The Seven Mysteries in the First Epistle of John,* pp. 68-70)

Further Reading: Life-study of Matthew, msgs. 10, 70; *Life-study of John,* msg. 37

Enlightenment and inspiration: _____

_____

_____

_____

Morning Nourishment

1 John He who believes into the Son of God has the testi-
5:10-13 mony in himself; he who does not believe God has
made Him a liar because he has not believed in the
testimony which God has testified concerning His
Son. And this is the testimony, that God gave to us
eternal life and this life is in His Son. He who has the
Son has the life; he who does not have the Son of God
does not have the life. I have written these things to
you that you may know that you have eternal life, to
you who believe into the name of the Son of God.

The water of baptism terminates the old creation, and the
blood shed on the cross redeems whatever God has chosen of the
old creation. Then the Spirit comes to germinate what God has
chosen and redeemed. Therefore, here we have termination,
redemption, and germination. As the old creation, we have been
terminated. But as God's chosen ones we were first redeemed and
then germinated to be the new creation. This new creation is a
composition of God's children. (*Life-study of 1 John*, p. 323)

Today's Reading

Through the water of His baptism, through the blood of His
cross, and as the Spirit, Christ has been testified as the Son of
God. By these three steps He has also come into our spirit. This
means that by termination, redemption, and germination, Christ
is now within us. Hallelujah, we are a terminated, redeemed, and
germinated people!

The testimony of God [in 1 John 5:9] is the testimony by water,
blood, and the Spirit that Jesus is the Son of God. This testimony is
greater than that of men.

Verse 10 says, "He who believes into the Son of God has the
testimony in himself; he who does not believe God has made Him
a liar because he has not believed in the testimony which God has
testified concerning His Son." God testified concerning His Son that
we may believe in His Son and have His divine life. If we believe in
His Son, we receive and have His testimony in ourselves.

In 5:11 and 12 John continues, "And this is the testimony, that God gave to us eternal life and this life is in His Son. He who has the Son has the life; he who does not have the Son of God does not have the life." The testimony of God is not only that Jesus is His Son, but also that He gives to us eternal life, which is in His Son. His Son is the means to give us His eternal life, which is His goal with us. Because the life is in the Son (John 1:4) and the Son is the life (John 11:25; 14:6; Col. 3:4), the Son and the life are one, inseparable. If we have the Son of God, we have eternal life, because eternal life is in the Son.

In 5:13 John says, "I have written these things to you that you may know that you have eternal life, to you who believe into the name of the Son of God."...Our believing to receive eternal life is the fact; the words of the Holy Writings are the assurance concerning this fact. They are the title deed of our eternal salvation. We are assured and have the pledge by them that because we believe in the name of the Son of God we have eternal life. (*Life-study of 1 John,* pp. 324-326)

Why do we need the witness of the Spirit? The Spirit germinates. We have been terminated, but we were also marked out before the foundation of the world. Because God chose us, He redeemed us. However, we were lifeless because of being terminated. When the Spirit came, He caused the seed to germinate. The seed is the Son of God. Today we are living, moving, and behaving in the Spirit. The Holy Spirit today is the Spirit of life. This life is the germinating seed within.

In the proper church life there must be a germination. We cannot remain the same. Even after two weeks, there is a difference. After two months there will be a bigger difference. There will be a steady growth in life. The church practice is to terminate people, to get them redeemed, and to germinate them! (*The Seven Mysteries in the First Epistle of John,* pp. 71-72)

Further Reading: Life-study of 1 John, msg. 40; A General Sketch of the New Testament in the Light of Christ and the Church, Part 3, ch. 31

Enlightenment and inspiration: _____

_____

_____

_____

Morning Nourishment

1 John   If anyone sees his brother sinning a sin not unto
5:16-17 death, he shall ask and he will give life to him, to
         those sinning not unto death. There is a sin unto
         death; I do not say that he should make request
         concerning that. All unrighteousness is sin, and
         there is sin not unto death.
Rom.   So we who are many are one Body in Christ, and
12:5   individually members one of another.

[First John 5:14 begins with the word "and," which] connects the life in 5:4-13 to the fellowship in 5:14-17. In the former section we have received eternal life, and we have the written word as the assurance of this. Now John uses what he has written in 5:4-13 as a basis to show us that this eternal life can overcome death. We have received eternal life, and this life has been testified, proved, and pledged within us.

Perhaps you regarded 5:14-17 as verses concerning our prayer and God's answer to our prayer. Actually, John's intention in these verses is to show us that the eternal life within us can overcome death both in ourselves and in other members of the church. Eternal life swallows up death within us and death within other members. (*Life-study of 1 John*, p. 328)

Today's Reading

If one sees his brother sinning, John writes, "He shall ask and he will give life to him, to those sinning not unto death" (1 John 5:16)....How is it possible to give life to someone?...What does it mean to give him life? It means that I impart Christ to him. It is of no help to talk doctrines to him. He has sinned because he is short of life. When we are short of the Lord Jesus, we commit sin. Doctrine will not help us to overcome sin. Only one person can overcome sin, and that is the Lord Jesus. If we lose our temper, that is an indication that we are short of the Lord Jesus. We do not need a rebuke. We do not need to be told what we should do or should not do. We do not need to be told that we were wrong. The more we are condemned, the more our temper will rise. A rebuking reduces our measure of Christ. What we need is an addition of Him, not a reduction. We need more of Him imparted into us.

What short simple words John uses! "Give life to him"—a first grader can read this. Yet how marvelous is the expression, found nowhere else in the Bible! Some may protest that the Bible tells us to admonish and rebuke. It does, but this is not the word of the mending ministry here. Why is Christianity so degraded? One reason is that there are many to admonish but few to give life. What can mend today's broken situation? Only the life-giving mending ministry. Christianity's poor situation is due to the shortage of life.

In the church life we must learn to minister life. This is what is needed. Do not try other ways. No way of helping is better than that of ministering life.

You may raise the objection that you yourself are short of life; how can you minister it to others? You may indeed be short of life. Then what should you do? Do not go to admonish or rebuke. Do not even go to the other party. You yourself must turn to the Lord. "Lord, have mercy upon me. My brother is sinning; he needs the supply of life. He lacks life. But so do I, Lord. I don't have much life either. Have mercy upon us, but first have mercy upon me. I need more life. I must have more life."...When you yourself have the supply, then you can supply others.

We need to learn that when any brother or sister sins, this is a strong indication that he or she is short of life. To be of help, we must first check whether we have life. Do we have a surplus of life? Do we have more than we need? If not, we must wait on the Lord with prayer and fasting until we get the rich supply. Then we can minister from this supply to others.

Our need is to have a bigger portion of the Lord Jesus. Then we shall have a surplus to minister to others, a surplus not of knowledge or doctrine but of God. (*The Mending Ministry of John*, pp. 93-95)

Further Reading: Life-study of 1 John, msg. 37; The Mending Ministry of John, ch. 11

Enlightenment and inspiration: _____

_____
_____
_____

Morning Nourishment

1 John   And this is the boldness which we have toward Him,
5:14-15   that if we ask anything according to His will, He
hears us. And if we know that He hears us in whatever we ask, we know that we have the requests
which we have asked from Him.

John   If you abide in Me and My words abide in you, ask
15:7   whatever you will, and it shall be done for you.

First John 5:4-13 shows us that we have received eternal life, as mentioned in 1:1-2. Then verses 14 through 17 tell us how we pray in the fellowship of eternal life, as mentioned in 1:3-7....In 5:14-17 we are in the fellowship of this life. Of course, the word "fellowship" is not here. These verses speak of prayer. When we pray by the divine life, we are in the fellowship of the divine life. Therefore, these verses in fact refer to the divine fellowship. (*Life-study of 1 John*, p. 327)

Today's Reading

In 1 John 5:14 John says, "This is the boldness which we have toward Him, that if we ask anything according to His will, He hears us." Here "boldness" refers to the boldness we have for our prayer in fellowship with God. Based upon the fact that we have received eternal life through the divine birth by believing in the Son of God, we can pray, in the fellowship of eternal life, by contacting God, in the boldness of a conscience void of offense (Acts 24:16), according to His will, with the assurance that He will hear us.

The prayer that is according to the will of God indicates that the praying one is abiding in the fellowship of the divine life and is also abiding in the Lord Himself. Such a believer is one with the Lord. This makes it possible to have boldness toward God. When we are in the fellowship of the divine life and our conscience is without offense, we have peace with God, and we also have boldness to pray, not according to our feeling, but according to His will. Because we pray according to His will, He hears us.

In 5:15 John goes on to say, "And if we know that He hears us in whatever we ask, we know that we have the requests which we have asked from Him." This knowing is based upon the fact that after having received the divine life, we abide in the Lord and are one with Him in our prayer to God in His name (John 15:7, 16; 16:23-24). Based upon the fact that we have received the divine life through the divine birth, we may abide in the Lord and be one with Him in our prayer. Because we are one with the Lord in prayer, we pray in His name. By this we know that He hears us in whatever we ask. Our asking is not in ourselves according to our mind, but in the Lord according to God's will. Therefore, we know that we have the requests which we have asked from Him....In both cases "he" refers to the same person, that is, to the one who sees his brother sinning and who asks concerning him.

The subject of "will give life" is still "he," the subject of the first predicate "shall ask." This indicates that the asker will give life to the one asked for. This does not mean that the asker has life of himself and can give life by himself to others. It means such an asker, who is abiding in the Lord, who is one with the Lord, and who is asking in one spirit with the Lord (1 Cor. 6:17), becomes the means through which God's life-giving Spirit can give life to the one he asks for. This is a matter of life-imparting in the fellowship of the divine life. To be one who can give life to others, we must abide in the divine life and walk, live, and have our being in the divine life. In James 5:14-16 the prayer is for healing; here the prayer is for life-imparting.

The vital point here is that if we would pray for a brother according to what is described in verse 16, we need to be one with the Lord. We must abide in the Lord and ask in one spirit with Him. Because we are so one with the Lord, we can become the means, the channel, through which God's life-giving Spirit can impart life to the one for whom we ask. This imparting of life takes place in the fellowship of the divine life. (*Life-study of 1 John*, pp. 329-331)

Further Reading: Life-study of John, msgs. 34, 37

Enlightenment and inspiration: Must be in fervent prayer blc the Lord, and be one with Him in prayer, Because we are one with the Lord in prayer, we pray in His name.

Morning Nourishment

John   And in that day you will ask Me nothing. Truly, truly,
16:23-24 I say to you, Whatever you ask the Father in My
         name, He will give to you. Until now you have asked
         for nothing in My name; ask and you shall receive,
         that your joy may be made full.
Amos   Surely the Lord Jehovah will not do anything unless
3:7   He reveals His secret to His servants the prophets.

What is described in 1 John 5:14-17 concerning the life-giving petition can be experienced only by those who are deep in the Lord. In verse 14 John speaks of prayer that is according to God's will. In order to pray this kind of prayer, we must be one with the Lord. If we are deeply one with Him, we shall know His will, and we shall also know the situation of the one who is sinning. Because this one is our brother, someone very close to us in the Lord, we shall know his real situation before the Lord. This matter is deep. (*Life-study of 1 John,* p. 337)

Today's Reading

If you are one with the Lord and know a sinning brother's condition and situation before the Lord, you will then know the Lord's will and be able to pray according to His will [1 John 5:14-17]. Because you know the Lord's will, you will also know whether or not this brother will die because of his sin.

These verses indicate that we who have eternal life can pass this life on to others. This means that we can be a channel through which eternal life is supplied to others. We can be a channel for eternal life to flow out of us and into others. Verse 16 refers to this. In this verse the one who asks is also the one who gives life to the sinning brother. This indicates that the one who asks will give life to the one concerning whom he asks. The asker, who is abiding in the Lord, who is one with the Lord, and who is asking in one spirit with the Lord, becomes the means through which God's life-giving Spirit can give life to the one for whom he asks. This is a matter of life-imparting in the fellowship of the divine life.

Notice that in verse 16 John speaks of someone seeing "his brother" sinning. The words "his brother" point to a brother who is close to him, someone who is so close to him that he is a part of him. If you have a brother close to you in this way and do not know whether this brother will die because of his sin, then you are not deep in the Lord. If you are truly deep in the Lord and are one with Him, as you consider the brother's situation, you will enter into the Lord's heart and know His will. You will know whether this brother, who is so intimate to you, will die because of his sin. Then you will know how to pray for him. You will know whether or not to pray for him to be forgiven and healed. If this brother's sin is unto death, you will realize that you should not pray to impart life into him. Instead, you may be burdened to pray for him from another angle.

My burden in this message is to show you that the eternal life within us is real and practical. On the one hand, we can enjoy this eternal life within us. On the other hand, we can pass on this eternal life to others. We can be a channel for eternal life to flow out from us, or through us, to others. However, the experience of being a channel for eternal life to flow out to others is a deep matter. This cannot be done in a superficial way. If we would be a channel for eternal life to flow out to others, we must be deep in the Lord, and we must know the Lord's heart by being in His heart. If we have entered into the Lord to such a degree, spontaneously we shall know the Lord's will concerning a brother close to us who has sinned. Because we know the Lord's will concerning the brother's situation, we shall know how to pray for him.

If there is the anointing, we should go on to pray for a brother according to the anointing. But if there is no anointing, we may be praying in ourselves. When we have these experiences, we know that eternal life is real and practical. (*Life-study of 1 John*, pp. 337-339)

Further Reading: Life-study of 1 John, msgs. 38-39

Enlightenment and inspiration: _____

_____

_____

_____

Hymns, #780

1 Praying always in the spirit,
  Never in the flesh or mind!
If this secret we will practise,
  God's full presence we will find.

    Praying always in the spirit
    Is the secret we are told!
    In the spirit, God to contact,
    Is the secret we must hold!

2 Praying always in the spirit,
  Never by our human thought!
Fellowship with God the Spirit
Only thus to us is brought.

3 Praying always in the spirit,
  Thus expressing God's desire;
Staying with the Lord in spirit,
  We'll be wholly set afire.

4 Praying always in the spirit,
  Even groaning from within,
Thus we utter God's intention
  By the Spirit's discipline.

5 Praying always in the spirit,
  In the holiest place divine;
It is only in the spirit
  God and we in oneness twine.

6 Praying always in the spirit,
  'Tis the only way of prayer;
All the fulness of the Godhead
  By this secret we may share.

Composition for prophecy with main point and sub-points:

God is faithful - He cannot ask us to do something He has equipped us for. Eternal life is within us. We have to stay in fellowship with the Lord constantly. Must have the vertical relationship (God) before we can have the horizontal (the saints) fellowship to be able to impart life to one another. A Mother cannot give milk to her Baby if she does not have any. We Must must be in intimate fellowship with God. Abide with him, Be one with Him, then we can impart life to our sinning brethren.

Lord I turn myself to you, Lord have mercy on me, My Sister (brother is sinning) he needs me life.

The eternal life within us is real and practical. God wants a corporate put. His life of expression. See (A) - see page 221. We need to read, pray and enjoy the Lord's word. When we come together, then we can impart life to one another.

Create a vital group - through calling & abiding constantly in the fellowship of Christ - and be able to discern other saints sin's and problems then we can turn to the Lord and pray and impart life to that saint.

See (B) - page 219. Preaching the gospel is imparting life to others. When we live, walk and fellowship with God → spontaneously the Lord's life will flow and supply life to others. -

**The True God as the Eternal Life
and the Seven Issues of the Seven Mysteries
in the First Epistle of John**

Scripture Reading: 1 John 2:12-14; 4:4; 5:4-5, 18, 20-21;
2 John 7, 9-11; 3 John 9-10

Day 1 I. **The Son of God has come and has given us
an understanding so that we might know
the true One, the genuine and real God
(1 John 5:20):**

A. This understanding is the faculty of our mind
enlightened and empowered by the Spirit of
reality to apprehend the divine reality in our
regenerated spirit (Eph. 4:23; John 16:12-15).

B. *Know* in 1 John 5:20 is the ability of the divine
life to know the true God in our regenerated
spirit through our renewed mind, enlightened
by the Spirit of reality (John 17:3; Eph. 1:17).

C. In 1 John 5:20 *Him who is true*—or *the true
One*—refers to God becoming subjective to us, to
the God who is objective becoming the true One
in our life and experience:

1. The true One is the divine reality; to know
the true One means to know the divine reality by experiencing, enjoying, and possessing this reality.

2. This indicates that the divine reality—God
Himself, who was once objective to us—has
become our subjective reality in our experience (v. 6).

Day 2 D. To be in the true One is to be in His Son Jesus
Christ (v. 20):

1. This indicates that Jesus Christ, the Son of
God, is the true God.

2. This also indicates that the true One and
Jesus Christ are one in the way of coinherence; thus, to be in the Son is to be in the
true One.

E. The word *this* in verse 20 refers to the God who
   has come through incarnation and has given us
   the ability to know Him as the genuine God and
   to be one with Him organically in His Son Jesus
   Christ:
   1. This genuine and real God is eternal life to
      us so that we may partake of Him as every-
      thing for our regenerated being.
   2. *This* refers to the true God and Jesus Christ
      in whom we are; it includes the fact that we
      are in this One, the true One, and implies
      that, in a practical sense, eternal life is the
      God in whom we are experientially.
   3. Therefore, the true God and eternal life
      include our being in the true One and in His
      Son Jesus Christ; now in our experience the
      true One becomes the true God, and Jesus
      Christ becomes eternal life.

Day 3 II. **The Epistles of John reveal the seven issues
        of the seven mysteries in 1 John: life (1:1-7),
        fellowship (vv. 3, 5-10), abiding (2:5-6, 24, 27-28;
        3:24), the anointing (2:20, 27), the divine birth
        (v. 29; 3:9; 4:7; 5:1), the divine seed (3:9), and
        the water, the blood, and the Spirit (5:6-9):**
        A. There will be distinctions in the level of life in
           the church life (2:12-14):
           1. There will be the growth in life that brings
              in the distinctions in life between the young
              children, the young men, and the fathers.
           2. If there is no growth in life, the believers
              will all be on the same level as far as life is
              concerned.
        B. There will be a strong testimony of victory—the
           testimony that the One who is in us is greater
           than the one who is in the world (4:4):
           1. The One who is in the believers is the Tri-
              une God, who dwells in them as the all-
              inclusive, life-giving, anointing Spirit and
              who strengthens them from within with all

the rich elements of the Triune God (Eph. 3:16-19).

2. *He who is in the world* is Satan, the evil spirit; such a one is lesser and weaker than the Triune God.

Day 4

C. We will overcome the world (1 John 5:4-5):

1. The regenerated believers have the capability of the divine life to overcome the world, the powerful satanic world system (v. 5; 2:15).

2. The regenerated spirit of the regenerated believer overcomes the world; the believer's divine birth with the divine life is the basic factor for such victorious living (5:4).

D. We will not be touched by the evil one (v. 18):

1. *The evil one* refers to one who is pernicious, harmfully evil, one who affects others, influencing them to be evil and vicious; such an evil one is Satan, the devil, in whom the whole world lies (v. 19).

2. A regenerated believer (especially his regenerated spirit, which is born of the Spirit of God—John 3:6) keeps himself from living in sin, and the evil one does not touch him (especially his regenerated spirit):

a. Whether or not we are under Satan's authority is not determined by what we do; it is determined by whether we are in the Spirit or in the flesh (Gal. 5:16-17).

b. As long as we remain in the mingled spirit—the regenerated human spirit mingled with the divine Spirit as one spirit—we will be kept, and Satan will have no way with us (1 Cor. 6:17; 1 John 5:18).

Day 5

E. We will not have idols (v. 21):

1. *Idols* refer to the heretical substitutes for the true God and to anything that replaces the true God, the subjective God, the God

whom we have experienced and are still experiencing (4:13-15).

2. An idol is anything that replaces the true God, the Triune God experienced by us as our life in a practical way (5:20).

F. We will reject the antichrists (2 John 7, 9-11; 1 John 2:18, 22):

1. An antichrist is one who denies Christ's deity, denying that Jesus is the Christ, that is, denying the Father and the Son by denying that Jesus is the Son of God, not confessing that He has come in the flesh through the divine conception of the Holy Spirit (v. 23; 4:2-3).

Day 6

2. The principle of antichrist is to deny some aspect of Christ's person and to replace it with something other than Christ (2:18).

G. We will not follow the divisive ones (3 John 9-10):

1. Diotrephes loved to be first; this is self-exaltation in one's actions (v. 9).

2. Diotrephes dominated the church in which he was, rejecting the apostles and some good saints and even casting out of the church those who received these saints (v. 10).

3. The cause of division is mainly rivalry for leadership; if we refuse to follow self-appointed leaders, there will not be any division (Luke 22:24-27).

Morning Nourishment

John 17:2-3 Even as You have given Him authority over all flesh to give eternal life to all whom You have given Him. And this is eternal life, that they may know You, the only true God, and Him whom You have sent, Jesus Christ.

1 John 5:20 And we know that the Son of God has come and has given us an understanding that we might know Him who is true; and we are in Him who is true, in His Son Jesus Christ. This is the true God and eternal life.

In 1 John 5:20 John says that the Son of God has given us an understanding that we might know Him who is true, or know the true One. This understanding is the faculty of our mind enlightened and empowered by the Spirit of reality (John 16:12-15) to apprehend the divine reality in our regenerated spirit....."Know" [here] is the ability of the divine life to know the true God (John 17:3) in our regenerated spirit (Eph. 1:17) through our renewed mind, enlightened by the Spirit of reality.

We have an enlightened mind and a quickened spirit with the Spirit of reality, who reveals spiritual reality to us. As a result, surely we have an understanding and are able to know the true One. Before we were saved, we did not have this understanding. But the Son of God has come to us and has given us this understanding so that we may know God. (*Life-study of 1 John,* pp. 348-349)

Today's Reading

In order to know God, the divine person, we need the divine life. Because as believers we have been born of the divine life, we are able to know God. In order to know a certain living thing, you need to have the life of that thing....It takes human life to know human beings. The principle is the same with knowing God. The Lord has given us eternal life, the divine life, the life of God....The life of God, which has been given to us, has the ability to know God and the things of God.

This Epistle reveals clearly that we have received the divine life, for we have been born of Him. Just as a child can know his father because he has the father's life, so we can know God because we have God's life. Having the divine life, we have the ability to know God. Because we have the life of God, we are able to experience God, enjoy God, and possess God.

The Son of God has come through incarnation and through death and resurrection and has given us an understanding, the ability to know the true God. This understanding includes our enlightened mind, our quickened spirit, and the revealing Holy Spirit. Because our mind has been enlightened, our spirit has been enlivened, and the Spirit of reality dwells in us, we have the ability to know God, the ability to experience, enjoy, and possess the true One.

In 1 John 5:20 John twice speaks of "Him who is true." A better translation would be "the true One." To speak of God simply as God may be to speak in a rather objective way. However, the term "the true One" is subjective; it refers to God becoming subjective to us. In this verse, the God who is objective becomes the true One in our life and experience.

What is the meaning of the expression "the true One"? In particular, what does the word "true" mean? Here the Greek word translated "true" is *alethinos,* genuine, real (an adjective akin to *aletheia,* truth, verity, reality—John 1:14; 14:6, 17), opposite of false and counterfeit. Actually, the true One is the reality. The Son of God has given us an understanding so that we may know— that is, experience, enjoy, and possess—this divine reality. Therefore, to know the true One means to know the reality by experiencing, enjoying, and possessing this reality.

First John 5:20 indicates that God has become our reality in our experience. The Son of God has come through incarnation and through death and resurrection and has given us an understanding so that we may experience, enjoy, and possess the reality, which is God Himself. Now the God who once was objective to us has become our subjective reality. (*Life-study of 1 John,* pp. 349-350, 351-352)

Further Reading: Life-study of 1 John, msg. 39; *Living in the Spirit,* ch. 5

Enlightenment and inspiration: _____

_____

_____

_____

Morning Nourishment

Col. **For in Him dwells all the fullness of the Godhead**
2:9 **bodily.**
Eph. **That the God of our Lord Jesus Christ, the Father**
1:17 **of glory, may give to you a spirit of wisdom and rev-**
elation in the full knowledge of Him.
1 John **And this is the testimony, that God gave to us eter-**
5:11 **nal life and this life is in His Son.**

In 1 John 5:20 John says that we are in the true One. We
not only know the true God; we are also in Him. We not only
have the knowledge of Him; we are in an organic union with
Him. We are one with Him organically.

When John says that we are in the true One, he is making
a crucial point. Not only do we know the true One, and not
only do we experience, enjoy, and possess Him as the reality,
but we are in this reality. We are in the true One.

In 5:20 John says, "We are in Him who is true, in His Son
Jesus Christ." To be in the true God is to be in His Son Jesus
Christ. Since Jesus Christ as the Son of God is the very
embodiment of God (Col. 2:9), to be in Him is to be in the true
God. This indicates that Jesus Christ the Son of God is the
true God. (*Life-study of 1 John*, p. 352)

Today's Reading

The true One and Jesus Christ are one in the way of
coinherence. Therefore, to be in the Son is spontaneously to be
in the true One. If "in His Son Jesus Christ" is a modifier, the
meaning is that we are in the true One by being in His Son
Jesus Christ. How are we in the true One? We are in Him by
being in His Son Jesus Christ.

If we consider this matter carefully, we shall see that in
both ways of understanding these phrases, the meaning is
actually the same. Whether we say that to be in the true One
is to be in His Son Jesus Christ, or we are in the true One by
virtue of being in Jesus Christ, the outcome is the same.

Let us now go on to consider the last part of 1 John 5:20:

"This is the true God and eternal life." "This" refers to the God who has come through incarnation and has given us the ability to know Him as the genuine God and be one with Him organically in His Son Jesus Christ. All this is the genuine and real God and eternal life to us. This genuine and real God is eternal life to us so that we may partake of Him as everything for our regenerated being.

We need to pay special attention to the word "this." In 5:20 John does not say "He is"; he says "This is." This is the correct translation of the Greek. Furthermore, John uses the word "this" to refer both to the true God and to eternal life. By this we see that the true God and eternal life are one.

We have seen that we are in the true One and in His Son Jesus Christ. Doctrinally, the true One and His Son Jesus Christ may be considered two. But when we are in the true One and in Jesus Christ experientially, They are one. For this reason John uses "this" to refer both to the true One and to His Son Jesus Christ.

When we are in Them, They become the true God and eternal life. We need a clear understanding of what "this" in 5:20 refers to. The word "this" refers to the very God who has become experiential to us through our being in Him. No longer are we outside of this God. Rather, we are in this God, and we are in the true One, in His Son Jesus Christ. Because we are in Them, God and Jesus Christ are no longer objective to us, and in our experience They are no longer two. When we are in Them, They become one to us. Therefore, John says that "this" is the true God, and "this" is eternal life. Who is "this"? "This" is the very God and the very Jesus Christ in whom we are. We may also say that "this" includes the condition of our being in God and Jesus Christ. Hence, the true God and eternal life include our being in the true One and His Son Jesus Christ. (*Life-study of 1 John,* pp. 353-355)

Further Reading: Life-study of 1 John, msgs. 36, 40

Enlightenment and inspiration: _____

_____

_____

_____

A-11

Morning Nourishment

1 John 2:12-14 I write to you, little children, because your sins have been forgiven you because of His name. I write to you, fathers, because you know Him who is from the beginning. I write to you, young men, because you have overcome the evil one. I write to you, young children, because you know the Father. I have written to you, fathers, because you know Him who is from the beginning. I have written to you, young men, because you are strong and the word of God abides in you and you have overcome the evil one.

4:4 You are of God, little children; and you have overcome them because greater is He who is in you than he who is in the world.

[There are] seven issues that result from the seven mysteries. First, there will be the growth that brings in the distinctions in life between the little ones, the young ones, and the fathers. Second, there will be a strong testimony of victory over the evil one. Third, the church will rise up out of the world. Fourth, Satan will not dare to touch the church. Fifth, we shall keep ourselves from idols. Sixth, we shall have nothing to do with antichrists. Seventh, we shall not give a following to divisive ones.

These issues are the outcome of life. They cannot be brought about by regulations. They result from our being in the reality of the seven mysteries: life; fellowship; abiding; the anointing; the divine birth; the divine seed; and the water, the blood, and the Spirit. (*The Seven Mysteries in the First Epistle of John*, p. 79)

Today's Reading

If we are in the reality of [the seven mysteries in 1 John], there will be seven things which characterize us....There should be growth in the church life. It is all too common for Christians to remain the same year after year. If we are still the way we were ten years ago, all of us will be on the same level as far as life is concerned. This is a poor situation and indicates a lack of growth. Among us there should be fathers, young men, and little children.

In the church life we should be able to see three stages of growth. New ones should be born in our midst—little children, who know the Father (2:13). As in a family, we love, care for, and protect these little ones, who are lively and even sometimes naughty. But we need also those on another level—young men, strong enough to fight the enemy and guard the church against any attacks. They should be strong in the Word, able to resist the world, the satanic system which frustrates people from God's purpose and from enjoying Him. Finally, we must also have those on the highest level—the fathers, who keep going back to the beginning.

That which was from the beginning is the eternal life. The Son of God as the life-giving Spirit is the origin of all things. The origin of the church, of holiness, of our new birth, and of our growth is life. Because of their experience, the fathers in the church have learned to stay with life. When others go to them to argue about doctrines or to get help with a problem in their family relationships, the fathers always bring these inquiring ones back to life.

To have these three levels in the church life is one issue of the seven mysteries....In the church [there are] some lively and living new ones, some strong, vigilant young men, and some fathers rich in life. (*The Seven Mysteries in the First Epistle of John,* pp. 73-74)

In 4:4, John tells the believers that He who is in them is greater than he who is in the world. [This is the second issue of the seven mysteries in 1 John.] The One in the believers is the Triune God, who dwells in the believers as the all-inclusive, life-giving, anointing Spirit and who strengthens us from within with all the rich elements of the Triune God (Eph. 3:16-19). Such a One is much greater and stronger than Satan, the evil spirit.

Satan usurps fallen mankind as the evil spirit and operates in evil persons, who are the components of his world system. Such a one is less than the Triune God and weaker than He is. (*Life-study of 1 John,* p. 292)

Further Reading: The Seven Mysteries in the First Epistle of John,
   ch. 9; *Life-study of 1 John,* msg. 19

Enlightenment and inspiration: All the believers are the little children. The 7 mysteries is for our daily living and brings us into the divine life (remain in the abiding) and sensitive with the growth. All operating in the divine life. Christ is in us as the growing to result

Morning Nourishment

1 John For everything that has been begotten of God over-
5:4-5 comes the world; and this is the victory which has
        overcome the world—our faith. And who is he who
        overcomes the world except him who believes that
        Jesus is the Son of God?
    18 We know that everyone who is begotten of God does
        not sin, but he who has been begotten of God keeps
        himself, and the evil one does not touch him.

[The third issue of practicing the seven mysteries in 1 John is that] there will be no place for the world. Without being exhorted not to love the world, the church will nonetheless find that the world has no hold on it. Because it contains the divine seed of life, the church will have no part in the world. The distinction goes further than not loving the world.

The keeping or guarding mentioned [in 1 John 5:4 and 18] is mainly from the world. The world is a satanic system which has ensnared everyone, including Christians. The only way out of this trap is by the life germ within us. (*The Seven Mysteries in the First Epistle of John,* pp. 74-75)

Today's Reading

If the church is practicing the seven mysteries,...[the saints] will be filled with life. They will hear the little word "no" time after time. When they go for a haircut, or when they go shopping, a voice within will say no to what they want. One of the most common words the Lord says to them is "no." When they eventually agree with this no and go along with the inner constraint, they will have an amen within. Then their response will be, "Praise the Lord!"

[This inner speaking comes] from life. There is no outward regulation, but Someone is within. This life is the substance of these mysteries. As the life grows, we shall...rise above, or grow out of, the world. We are the calamus plant, shooting out of the muddy situation into the clear sky. This is resurrection. When we look down from the heavens, we shall see how small, how pathetic, and how unlovely the world is. We shall wonder how we could ever have thought it attractive. Thus, the whole church will rise up from the world. (*The Seven Mysteries in the First Epistle of John,* p. 75)

In 1 John 5:18 John…is saying that as long as we abide in our regenerated spirit, this spirit will keep us from sinning, and the evil one does not touch us. He knows that if he tries to touch us when we are abiding in our regenerated spirit, he will be wasting his time. Hence, the thought here is not that the evil one cannot touch us, but that he does not touch us when we are in spirit.

We know from experience that when we are in the flesh, forgetting our regenerated spirit, we become prey to the evil one, even a "delicious dish" for him to eat. At such a time, the evil one may say, "Oh, here is something good for me to eat." The evil one will not only touch us—he will swallow us. But when we are in our regenerated spirit, he will not waste his time with us.

The thought in 5:18 is that we have been born of God and have the divine life. This divine birth took place in our regenerated spirit, and now the divine life is in our regenerated spirit. Therefore, we should simply stay in our regenerated spirit. Regeneration with the divine birth and the divine life keeps us from sin, failure, and defilement. When we stay in our regenerated spirit, Satan knows that there is no way for him to touch us, and he will not try to touch us.

If we consider the entire Epistle, we shall realize that the apostle John is trying to impress us with the fact that we have been born of God. We have had a divine birth, and we possess the divine life. A specific part of our being—our spirit—has been regenerated with the divine life. Now we have a safeguard: our regenerated spirit with the divine life. As long as we stay in our regenerated spirit, we are in a refuge, a place of protection and safeguard, and the evil one does not touch us. (*Life-study of 1 John,* pp. 346-347)

Further Reading: Life-study of 1 John, msg. 20; *The Collected Works of Watchman Nee,* vol. 39, pp. 59-75

Enlightenment and inspiration: _____

_____

_____

_____

Morning Nourishment

1 John   Young children, it is the last hour; and even as you
2:18   heard that antichrist is coming, even now many
         antichrists have come; whereby we know that it is
         the last hour.
   22   Who is the liar if not he who denies that Jesus is the
         Christ? This is the antichrist, the one who denies
         the Father and the Son.
5:21   Little children, guard yourselves from idols.

"Idols" [in 1 John 5:21] refers to the heretical substitutes, brought in by the Gnostics and Cerinthians, for the true God, as revealed in this Epistle and in John's Gospel and referred to in the preceding verse. Idols here also refer to anything that replaces the real God. We as genuine children of the genuine God should be on the alert to guard ourselves from these heretical substitutes and all vain replacements of our genuine and real God, with whom we are organically one and who is eternal life to us. This is the aged apostle's word of warning to all his little children as a conclusion of his Epistle. (*Life-study of 1 John*, p. 356)

Today's Reading

An idol is anything that replaces, is a substitute for, the subjective God, the God whom we have experienced and whom we are still experiencing. Through this enlightenment, we are able to understand 1 John 5:18-21 in a very experiential way.

Before we were saved, we were outside of God. God was true in Himself, but we could not say in our experience that He was true to us. But after we believed in the Lord Jesus, we entered into God. Therefore, 5:20 says not only that we know the true One, but also that we are in the true One....Because we are in God, He now experientially becomes true to us. Likewise, because we are in Jesus Christ, He becomes experientially true to us. Due to our experience of God and Christ by being in God and in Christ, we can say that this is the true God and eternal life.

God, Jesus Christ, and eternal life are one. In doctrine, there may be a distinction between God, Christ, and eternal life, but in our experience they are one. When we are in God and in Jesus Christ and when we experience eternal life, we find that all these are one. Therefore, John concludes verse 20 by saying, "This is the true God and eternal life." John's last word, in 5:21, is the charge to guard ourselves from idols. Anything that is a substitute or replacement for the true God and eternal life is an idol. We need to live, walk, and have our being in this God and in this life. If we do not live in the true God and eternal life, then we shall have a substitute for the true God, and this substitute will be an idol.

In 1 John 2:18 John says, "Young children, it is the last hour; and even as you heard that antichrist is coming, even now many antichrists have come; whereby we know that it is the last hour." An antichrist differs from a false Christ (Matt. 24:5, 24). A false Christ is one who pretends to be the Christ in a deceiving way, whereas an antichrist is one who denies Christ's deity, denying that Jesus is the Christ, that is, denying the Father and the Son by denying that Jesus is the Son of God (vv. 22-23), not confessing that He has come in the flesh through the divine conception of the Holy Spirit (4:2-3). At the time of the apostle John, many heretics, like the Gnostics, Cerinthians, and Docetists, taught heresies concerning the Person of Christ, that is, concerning His divinity and humanity.

In verse 19 John goes on to say, "They went out from us, but they were not of us; for if they had been of us, they would have remained with us; but they went out that they might be manifested that they all are not of us." These antichrists were not born of God and were not in the fellowship of the apostles with the believers (1:3; Acts 2:42). Hence, they were not of the church, that is, not of the Body of Christ. To remain with the apostles and the believers is to remain in the fellowship of the Body of Christ. (*Life-study of 1 John*, pp. 356-357, 204-205)

Further Reading: Life-study of 1 John, msg. 24; Life-study of 2 John, msg. 2

Enlightenment and inspiration: _____

_____

_____

_____

Morning Nourishment

3 John   I wrote something to the church; but Diotrephes, who
9-10   loves to be first among them, does not receive us. For
this reason, if I come, I will bring to remembrance his
works which he does, babbling against us with evil
words; and not being satisfied with these, neither does
he himself receive the brothers, and those intending
to *do so* he forbids and casts out of the church.

2 John   For many deceivers went out into the world, those
7   who do not confess Jesus Christ coming in the flesh.
This is the deceiver and the antichrist.

The principle of antichrist involves denying what Christ is. This is to be anti-Christ, against Christ. Of course, whenever someone denies what Christ is, automatically that person will replace Christ with something else. Hence, an antichrist is both against Christ and is one who replaces Christ.

Modernists deny that Christ is the Redeemer who died on the cross for our sins. First, they deny this aspect of Christ's person. Then they go on to replace the Redeemer with a martyr….This is to have something instead of Christ as the result of denying what Christ is.

We should never deny any part, any aspect, or any item of Christ's person. To deny any aspect of Christ's person is to practice the principle of antichrist….One may not be against Christ or deny Christ consciously. But unconsciously we may deny some aspect of Christ's person and then replace this aspect with something else. (*Life-study of 1 John*, pp. 272-273)

Today's Reading

Among Christians today…two problems still exist. The first problem, the desire to be above others in thought, is related to doctrine. The second problem, the love of being first, is related to practice. In doctrine many desire to be advanced, to go beyond others. In practice, many love to be first. Such a love leads even to the desire to be a "pope." Sometimes this evil principle creeps into the church life. For example, in standing up to give a testimony we may want to say something advanced, something that goes beyond what others can say. Furthermore, in the church life we may also desire to be first. Even in a small service group, we may want to be the first, the head. This is in principle the evil spirit of Diotrephes. Diotrephes...advocated, promoted, Gnosticism. In this we see the subtlety of the enemy in trying to annul the enjoyment of the Triune God. Satan in his subtlety seeks either to distract us from the enjoyment of the Triune God, to cut us off from this enjoyment, or even to destroy it altogether. Consider the situation among believers today with respect to the enjoyment of the Triune God. Even the teaching of the Bible is utilized by the enemy to keep believers away from the proper enjoyment of the Triune God. Concerning this matter, a battle is raging, and we are fighting for the truth. We are not fighting for doctrine; we are fighting for the reality, which is the enjoyment of the Triune God. (*Life-study of 3 John*, pp. 12-13)

Whether Diotrephes was a real Christian I do not know, but he was one who loved to have the first place in the church. He was one who dominated the church in which he was, rejecting the apostles and some good saints and even casting out of the church those who received these saints. You may think he is an extreme case, but the same thing is still existing today.

What is the cause of division? It is mainly because of the rivalry for the leadership. "I want to be the head. I will not be under you. If I am not number one, I will set up another group so that I can be in charge." No one, of course, will openly make such a declaration. He will wear a beautiful cloak and hide behind it if accused of causing division. But as a church, full of life, we can see through his outward pretense. Thus, we reject both antichrist and Diotrephes. If we refuse to follow self-appointed leaders, there will not be any division. Christ is our only Head. (*The Seven Mysteries in the First Epistle of John*, pp. 78-79)

Further Reading: Life-study of 1 John, msgs. 31, 33; Life-study of 3 John, msg. 2

Enlightenment and inspiration: _____

_____
_____
_____

Hymns, #1247

1   If our hearts would be established;
    If in spirit we would be;
    If we would be overcomers;
    Follow Jesus constantly.

      Follow Jesus in the spirit;
      Be the overcomers true;
      Follow Jesus every moment—
      Jesus, help us follow You.

2   If we would be built together;
    If related we would be;
    To be fitly framed together;
    Follow brothers constantly.

      Follow brothers for the building;
      Never independent be;
      Follow brothers, be in order,
      Functioning in harmony.

3   If we're for the Lord's recovery;
    If the earth the Lord's would be;
    If we would bring in the kingdom;
    Follow churches constantly.

      Follow all the local churches;
      Thus, the kingdom we will see.
      Follow in the churches' flowing
      For the Lord's recovery.

4   We would all be better followers,
    Taking in with joy the Word;
    It enables us to follow
    Brothers, churches, and our Lord.

      Follow Jesus; follow brothers;
      Follow churches in the flow;
      By the Word of God amening
      We can all attain this goal.

Composition for prophecy with main point and sub-points: We must remain in the enjoyment of the Lord in order to defeat Satan.

The regenerated believer have the capability of the divine life to overcome the world, the powerful satanic world system. The regenerated spirit of the regenerated believer overcomes the world; the believer's divine birth with the divine life is the basic factor for such victorious living;

We will not be touched by the evil one. As long as we remain in the mingled spirit - the regenerated human spirit mingled with the divine Spirit as one spirit - we will be kept, and Satan will have no way with as - Then we will be a strong testimony of victory - the testimony that the One who is in us is greater than he who is in the world. The One who is in the believers is the Triune God, who dwells in them as the all-inclusive, life-giving, anointing Spirit and who strengthens us from within with all the rich elements of the Triune God.

We need to deny ourselves, everything we do in the flesh (sin) destroys the church?

Reading Schedule for the Recovery Version of the Old Testament with Footnotes

Wk.	Lord's Day	Monday	Tuesday	Wednesday	Thursday	Friday	Saturday
1	☐ Gen 1:1-5	☐ 1:6-23	☐ 1:24-31	☐ 2:1-9	☐ 2:10-25	☐ 3:1-13	☐ 3:14-24
2	☐ 4:1-26	☐ 5:1-32	☐ 6:1-22	☐ 7:1—8:3	☐ 8:4-22	☐ 9:1-29	☐ 10:1-32
3	☐ 11:1-32	☐ 12:1-20	☐ 13:1-18	☐ 14:1-24	☐ 15:1-21	☐ 16:1-16	☐ 17:1-27
4	☐ 18:1-33	☐ 19:1-38	☐ 20:1-18	☐ 21:1-34	☐ 22:1-24	☐ 23:1—24:27	☐ 24:28-67
5	☐ 25:1-34	☐ 26:1-35	☐ 27:1-46	☐ 28:1-22	☐ 29:1-35	☐ 30:1-43	☐ 31:1-55
6	☐ 32:1-32	☐ 33:1—34:31	☐ 35:1-29	☐ 36:1-43	☐ 37:1-36	☐ 38:1—39:23	☐ 40:1—41:13
7	☐ 41:14-57	☐ 42:1-38	☐ 43:1-34	☐ 44:1-34	☐ 45:1-28	☐ 46:1-34	☐ 47:1-31
8	☐ 48:1-22	☐ 49:1-15	☐ 49:16-33	☐ 50:1-26	☐ Exo 1:1-22	☐ 2:1-25	☐ 3:1-22
9	☐ 4:1-31	☐ 5:1-23	☐ 6:1-30	☐ 7:1-25	☐ 8:1-32	☐ 9:1-35	☐ 10:1-29
10	☐ 11:1-10	☐ 12:1-14	☐ 12:15-36	☐ 12:37-51	☐ 13:1-22	☐ 14:1-31	☐ 15:1-27
11	☐ 16:1-36	☐ 17:1-16	☐ 18:1-27	☐ 19:1-25	☐ 20:1-26	☐ 21:1-36	☐ 22:1-31
12	☐ 23:1-33	☐ 24:1-18	☐ 25:1-22	☐ 25:23-40	☐ 26:1-14	☐ 26:15-37	☐ 27:1-21
13	☐ 28:1-21	☐ 28:22-43	☐ 29:1-21	☐ 29:22-46	☐ 30:1-10	☐ 30:11-38	☐ 31:1-17
14	☐ 31:18—32:35	☐ 33:1-23	☐ 34:1-35	☐ 35:1-35	☐ 36:1-38	☐ 37:1-29	☐ 38:1-31
15	☐ 39:1-43	☐ 40:1-38	☐ Lev 1:1-17	☐ 2:1-16	☐ 3:1-17	☐ 4:1-35	☐ 5:1-19
16	☐ 6:1-30	☐ 7:1-38	☐ 8:1-36	☐ 9:1-24	☐ 10:1-20	☐ 11:1-47	☐ 12:1-8
17	☐ 13:1-28	☐ 13:29-59	☐ 14:1-18	☐ 14:19-32	☐ 14:33-57	☐ 15:1-33	☐ 16:1-17
18	☐ 16:18-34	☐ 17:1-16	☐ 18:1-30	☐ 19:1-37	☐ 20:1-27	☐ 21:1-24	☐ 22:1-33
19	☐ 23:1-22	☐ 23:23-44	☐ 24:1-23	☐ 25:1-23	☐ 25:24-55	☐ 26:1-24	☐ 26:25-46
20	☐ 27:1-34	☐ Num 1:1-54	☐ 2:1-34	☐ 3:1-51	☐ 4:1-49	☐ 5:1-31	☐ 6:1-27
21	☐ 7:1-41	☐ 7:42-88	☐ 7:89—8:26	☐ 9:1-23	☐ 10:1-36	☐ 11:1-35	☐ 12:1—13:33
22	☐ 14:1-45	☐ 15:1-41	☐ 16:1-50	☐ 17:1—18:7	☐ 18:8-32	☐ 19:1-22	☐ 20:1-29
23	☐ 21:1-35	☐ 22:1-41	☐ 23:1-30	☐ 24:1-25	☐ 25:1-18	☐ 26:1-65	☐ 27:1-23
24	☐ 28:1-31	☐ 29:1-40	☐ 30:1—31:24	☐ 31:25-54	☐ 32:1-42	☐ 33:1-56	☐ 34:1-29
25	☐ 35:1-34	☐ 36:1-13	☐ Deut 1:1-46	☐ 2:1-37	☐ 3:1-29	☐ 4:1-49	☐ 5:1-33
26	☐ 6:1—7:26	☐ 8:1-20	☐ 9:1-29	☐ 10:1-22	☐ 11:1-32	☐ 12:1-32	☐ 13:1—14:21

Reading Schedule for the Recovery Version of the Old Testament with Footnotes

Wk.	Lord's Day	Monday	Tuesday	Wednesday	Thursday	Friday	Saturday
27	☐ 14:22—15:23	☐ 16:1-22	☐ 17:1—18:8	☐ 18:9—19:21	☐ 20:1—21:17	☐ 21:18—22:30	☐ 23:1-25
28	☐ 24:1-22	☐ 25:1-19	☐ 26:1-19	☐ 27:1-26	☐ 28:1-68	☐ 29:1-29	☐ 30:1—31:29
29	☐ 31:30—32:52	☐ 33:1-29	☐ 34:1-12	☐ Josh 1:1-18	☐ 2:1-24	☐ 3:1-17	☐ 4:1-24
30	☐ 5:1-15	☐ 6:1-27	☐ 7:1-26	☐ 8:1-35	☐ 9:1-27	☐ 10:1-43	☐ 11:1—12:24
31	☐ 13:1-33	☐ 14:1—15:63	☐ 16:1—18:28	☐ 19:1-51	☐ 20:1—21:45	☐ 22:1-34	☐ 23:1—24:33
32	☐ Judg 1:1-36	☐ 2:1-23	☐ 3:1-31	☐ 4:1-24	☐ 5:1-31	☐ 6:1-40	☐ 7:1-25
33	☐ 8:1-35	☐ 9:1-57	☐ 10:1—11:40	☐ 12:1—13:25	☐ 14:1—15:20	☐ 16:1-31	☐ 17:1—18:31
34	☐ 19:1-30	☐ 20:1-48	☐ 21:1-25	☐ Ruth 1:1-22	☐ 2:1-23	☐ 3:1-18	☐ 4:1-22
35	☐ 1 Sam 1:1-28	☐ 2:1-36	☐ 3:1—4:22	☐ 5:1—6:21	☐ 7:1—8:22	☐ 9:1-27	☐ 10:1—11:15
36	☐ 12:1—13:23	☐ 14:1-52	☐ 15:1-35	☐ 16:1-23	☐ 17:1-58	☐ 18:1-30	☐ 19:1-24
37	☐ 20:1-42	☐ 21:1—22:23	☐ 23:1—24:22	☐ 25:1-44	☐ 26:1-25	☐ 27:1—28:25	☐ 29:1—30:31
38	☐ 31:1-13	☐ 2 Sam 1:1-27	☐ 2:1-32	☐ 3:1-39	☐ 4:1—5:25	☐ 6:1-23	☐ 7:1-29
39	☐ 8:1—9:13	☐ 10:1—11:27	☐ 12:1-31	☐ 13:1-39	☐ 14:1-33	☐ 15:1—16:23	☐ 17:1—18:33
40	☐ 19:1-43	☐ 20:1—21:22	☐ 22:1-51	☐ 23:1-39	☐ 24:1-25	☐ 1 Kings 1:1-19	☐ 1:20-53
41	☐ 2:1-46	☐ 3:1-28	☐ 4:1-34	☐ 5:1—6:38	☐ 7:1-22	☐ 7:23-51	☐ 8:1-36
42	☐ 8:37-66	☐ 9:1-28	☐ 10:1-29	☐ 11:1-43	☐ 12:1-33	☐ 13:1-34	☐ 14:1-31
43	☐ 15:1-34	☐ 16:1—17:24	☐ 18:1-46	☐ 19:1-21	☐ 20:1-43	☐ 21:1—22:53	☐ 2 Kings 1:1-18
44	☐ 2:1—3:27	☐ 4:1-44	☐ 5:1—6:33	☐ 7:1-20	☐ 8:1-29	☐ 9:1-37	☐ 10:1-36
45	☐ 11:1—12:21	☐ 13:1—14:29	☐ 15:1-38	☐ 16:1-20	☐ 17:1-41	☐ 18:1-37	☐ 19:1-37
46	☐ 20:1—21:26	☐ 22:1-20	☐ 23:1-37	☐ 24:1—25:30	☐ 1 Chron 1:1-54	☐ 2:1—3:24	☐ 4:1—5:26
47	☐ 6:1-81	☐ 7:1-40	☐ 8:1-40	☐ 9:1-44	☐ 10:1—11:47	☐ 12:1-40	☐ 13:1—14:17
48	☐ 15:1—16:43	☐ 17:1-27	☐ 18:1—19:19	☐ 20:1—21:30	☐ 22:1—23:32	☐ 24:1—25:31	☐ 26:1-32
49	☐ 27:1-34	☐ 28:1—29:30	☐ 2 Chron 1:1-17	☐ 2:1—3:17	☐ 4:1—5:14	☐ 6:1-42	☐ 7:1—8:18
50	☐ 9:1—10:19	☐ 11:1—12:16	☐ 13:1—15:19	☐ 16:1—17:19	☐ 18:1—19:11	☐ 20:1-37	☐ 21:1—22:12
51	☐ 23:1—24:27	☐ 25:1—26:23	☐ 27:1—28:27	☐ 29:1-36	☐ 30:1—31:21	☐ 32:1-33	☐ 33:1—34:33
52	☐ 35:1—36:23	☐ Ezra 1:1-11	☐ 2:1-70	☐ 3:1—4:24	☐ 5:1—6:22	☐ 7:1-28	☐ 8:1-36

Reading Schedule for the Recovery Version of the Old Testament with Footnotes

Wk.	Lord's Day	Monday	Tuesday	Wednesday	Thursday	Friday	Saturday
53	☐ 9:1—10:44	☐ Neh 1:1-11	☐ 2:1—3:32	☐ 4:1—5:19	☐ 6:1-19	☐ 7:1-73	☐ 8:1-18
54	☐ 9:1-20	☐ 9:21-38	☐ 10:1—11:36	☐ 12:1-47	☐ 13:1-31	☐ Esth 1:1-22	☐ 2:1—3:15
55	☐ 4:1—5:14	☐ 6:1—7:10	☐ 8:1-17	☐ 9:1—10:3	☐ Job 1:1-22	☐ 2:1—3:26	☐ 4:1—5:27
56	☐ 6:1—7:21	☐ 8:1—9:35	☐ 10:1—11:20	☐ 12:1—13:28	☐ 14:1—15:35	☐ 16:1—17:16	☐ 18:1—19:29
57	☐ 20:1—21:34	☐ 22:1—23:17	☐ 24:1—25:6	☐ 26:1—27:23	☐ 28:1—29:25	☐ 30:1—31:40	☐ 32:1—33:33
58	☐ 34:1—35:16	☐ 36:1-33	☐ 37:1-24	☐ 38:1-41	☐ 39:1-30	☐ 40:1-24	☐ 41:1-34
59	☐ 42:1-17	☐ Psa 1:1-6	☐ 2:1—3:8	☐ 4:1—6:10	☐ 7:1—8:9	☐ 9:1—10:18	☐ 11:1—15:5
60	☐ 16:1—17:15	☐ 18:1-50	☐ 19:1—21:13	☐ 22:1-31	☐ 23:1—24:10	☐ 25:1—27:14	☐ 28:1—30:12
61	☐ 31:1—32:11	☐ 33:1—34:22	☐ 35:1—36:12	☐ 37:1-40	☐ 38:1—39:13	☐ 40:1—41:13	☐ 42:1—43:5
62	☐ 44:1-26	☐ 45:1-17	☐ 46:1—48:14	☐ 49:1—50:23	☐ 51:1—52:9	☐ 53:1—55:23	☐ 56:1—58:11
63	☐ 59:1—61:8	☐ 62:1—64:10	☐ 65:1—67:7	☐ 68:1-35	☐ 69:1—70:5	☐ 71:1—72:20	☐ 73:1—74:23
64	☐ 75:1—77:20	☐ 78:1-72	☐ 79:1—81:16	☐ 82:1—84:12	☐ 85:1—87:7	☐ 88:1—89:52	☐ 90:1—91:16
65	☐ 92:1—94:23	☐ 95:1—97:12	☐ 98:1—101:8	☐ 102:1—103:22	☐ 104:1—105:45	☐ 106:1-48	☐ 107:1-43
66	☐ 108:1—109:31	☐ 110:1—112:10	☐ 113:1—115:18	☐ 116:1—118:29	☐ 119:1-32	☐ 119:33-72	☐ 119:73-120
67	☐ 119:121-176	☐ 120:1—124:8	☐ 125:1—128:6	☐ 129:1—132:18	☐ 133:1—135:21	☐ 136:1—138:8	☐ 139:1—140:13
68	☐ 141:1—144:15	☐ 145:1—147:20	☐ 148:1—150:6	☐ Prov 1:1-33	☐ 2:1—3:35	☐ 4:1—5:23	☐ 6:1-35
69	☐ 7:1—8:36	☐ 9:1—10:32	☐ 11:1—12:28	☐ 13:1—14:35	☐ 15:1-33	☐ 16:1-33	☐ 17:1-28
70	☐ 18:1-24	☐ 19:1—20:30	☐ 21:1—22:29	☐ 23:1-35	☐ 24:1—25:28	☐ 26:1—27:27	☐ 28:1—29:27
71	☐ 30:1-33	☐ 31:1-31	☐ Eccl 1:1-18	☐ 2:1—3:22	☐ 4:1—5:20	☐ 6:1—7:29	☐ 8:1—9:18
72	☐ 10:1—11:10	☐ 12:1-14	☐ S.S 1:1-8	☐ 1:9-17	☐ 2:1-17	☐ 3:1-11	☐ 4:1-8
73	☐ 4:9-16	☐ 5:1-16	☐ 6:1-13	☐ 7:1-13	☐ 8:1-14	☐ Isa 1:1-11	☐ 1:12-31
74	☐ 2:1-22	☐ 3:1-26	☐ 4:1-6	☐ 5:1-30	☐ 6:1-13	☐ 7:1-25	☐ 8:1-22
75	☐ 9:1-21	☐ 10:1-34	☐ 11:1—12:6	☐ 13:1-22	☐ 14:1-14	☐ 14:15-32	☐ 15:1—16:14
76	☐ 17:1—18:7	☐ 19:1-25	☐ 20:1—21:17	☐ 22:1-25	☐ 23:1-18	☐ 24:1-23	☐ 25:1-12
77	☐ 26:1-21	☐ 27:1-13	☐ 28:1-29	☐ 29:1-24	☐ 30:1-33	☐ 31:1—32:20	☐ 33:1-24
78	☐ 34:1-17	☐ 35:1-10	☐ 36:1-22	☐ 37:1-38	☐ 38:1—39:8	☐ 40:1-31	☐ 41:1-29

Reading Schedule for the Recovery Version of the Old Testament with Footnotes

Wk.	Lord's Day	Monday	Tuesday	Wednesday	Thursday	Friday	Saturday
79	☐ 42:1-25	☐ 43:1-28	☐ 44:1-28	☐ 45:1-25	☐ 46:1-13	☐ 47:1-15	☐ 48:1-22
80	☐ 49:1-13	☐ 49:14-26	☐ 50:1—51:23	☐ 52:1-15	☐ 53:1-12	☐ 54:1-17	☐ 55:1-13
81	☐ 56:1-12	☐ 57:1-21	☐ 58:1-14	☐ 59:1-21	☐ 60:1-22	☐ 61:1-11	☐ 62:1-12
82	☐ 63:1-19	☐ 64:1-12	☐ 65:1-24	☐ 66:1-24	☐ Jer 1:1-19	☐ 2:1-19	☐ 2:20-37
83	☐ 3:1-25	☐ 4:1-31	☐ 5:1-31	☐ 6:1-30	☐ 7:1-34	☐ 8:1-22	☐ 9:1-26
84	☐ 10:1-25	☐ 11:1—12:17	☐ 13:1-27	☐ 14:1-22	☐ 15:1-21	☐ 16:1—17:27	☐ 18:1-23
85	☐ 19:1—20:18	☐ 21:1—22:30	☐ 23:1-40	☐ 24:1—25:38	☐ 26:1—27:22	☐ 28:1—29:32	☐ 30:1-24
86	☐ 31:1-23	☐ 31:24-40	☐ 32:1-44	☐ 33:1-26	☐ 34:1-22	☐ 35:1-19	☐ 36:1-32
87	☐ 37:1-21	☐ 38:1-28	☐ 39:1—40:16	☐ 41:1—42:22	☐ 43:1—44:30	☐ 45:1—46:28	☐ 47:1—48:16
88	☐ 48:17-47	☐ 49:1-22	☐ 49:23-39	☐ 50:1-27	☐ 50:28-46	☐ 51:1-27	☐ 51:28-64
89	☐ 52:1-34	☐ Lam 1:1-22	☐ 2:1-22	☐ 3:1-39	☐ 3:40-66	☐ 4:1-22	☐ 5:1-22
90	☐ Ezek 1:1-14	☐ 1:15-28	☐ 2:1—3:27	☐ 4:1—5:17	☐ 6:1—7:27	☐ 8:1—9:11	☐ 10:1—11:25
91	☐ 12:1—13:23	☐ 14:1—15:8	☐ 16:1-63	☐ 17:1—18:32	☐ 19:1-14	☐ 20:1-49	☐ 21:1-32
92	☐ 22:1-31	☐ 23:1-49	☐ 24:1-27	☐ 25:1—26:21	☐ 27:1-36	☐ 28:1-26	☐ 29:1—30:26
93	☐ 31:1—32:32	☐ 33:1-33	☐ 34:1-31	☐ 35:1—36:21	☐ 36:22-38	☐ 37:1-28	☐ 38:1—39:29
94	☐ 40:1-27	☐ 40:28-49	☐ 41:1-26	☐ 42:1—43:27	☐ 44:1-31	☐ 45:1-25	☐ 46:1-24
95	☐ 47:1-23	☐ 48:1-35	☐ Dan 1:1-21	☐ 2:1-30	☐ 2:31-49	☐ 3:1-30	☐ 4:1-37
96	☐ 5:1-31	☐ 6:1-28	☐ 7:1-12	☐ 7:13-28	☐ 8:1-27	☐ 9:1-27	☐ 10:1-21
97	☐ 11:1-22	☐ 11:23-45	☐ 12:1-13	☐ Hosea 1:1-11	☐ 2:1-23	☐ 3:1—4:19	☐ 5:1-15
98	☐ 6:1-11	☐ 7:1-16	☐ 8:1-14	☐ 9:1-17	☐ 10:1-15	☐ 11:1-12	☐ 12:1-14
99	☐ 13:1—14:9	☐ Joel 1:1-20	☐ 2:1-16	☐ 2:17-32	☐ 3:1-21	☐ Amos 1:1-15	☐ 2:1-16
100	☐ 3:1-15	☐ 4:1—5:27	☐ 6:1—7:17	☐ 8:1—9:15	☐ Obad 1-21	☐ Jonah 1:1-17	☐ 2:1—4:11
101	☐ Micah 1:1-16	☐ 2:1—3:12	☐ 4:1—5:15	☐ 6:1—7:20	☐ Nahum 1:1-15	☐ 2:1—3:19	☐ Hab 1:1-17
102	☐ 2:1-20	☐ 3:1-19	☐ Zeph 1:1-18	☐ 2:1-15	☐ 3:1-20	☐ Hag 1:1-15	☐ 2:1-23
103	☐ Zech 1:1-21	☐ 2:1-13	☐ 3:1-10	☐ 4:1-14	☐ 5:1—6:15	☐ 7:1—8:23	☐ 9:1-17
104	☐ 10:1—11:17	☐ 12:1—13:9	☐ 14:1-21	☐ Mal 1:1-14	☐ 2:1-17	☐ 3:1-18	☐ 4:1-6

Reading Schedule for the Recovery Version of the New Testament with Footnotes

Wk.	Lord's Day	Monday	Tuesday	Wednesday	Thursday	Friday	Saturday
1	☐ Matt 1:1-2	☐ 1:3-7	☐ 1:8-17	☐ 1:18-25	☐ 2:1-23	☐ 3:1-6	☐ 3:7-17
2	☐ 4:1-11	☐ 4:12-25	☐ 5:1-4	☐ 5:5-12	☐ 5:13-20	☐ 5:21-26	☐ 5:27-48
3	☐ 6:1-8	☐ 6:9-18	☐ 6:19-34	☐ 7:1-12	☐ 7:13-29	☐ 8:1-13	☐ 8:14-22
4	☐ 8:23-34	☐ 9:1-13	☐ 9:14-17	☐ 9:18-34	☐ 9:35—10:5	☐ 10:6-25	☐ 10:26-42
5	☐ 11:1-15	☐ 11:16-30	☐ 12:1-14	☐ 12:15-32	☐ 12:33-42	☐ 12:43—13:2	☐ 13:3-12
6	☐ 13:13-30	☐ 13:31-43	☐ 13:44-58	☐ 14:1-13	☐ 14:14-21	☐ 14:22-36	☐ 15:1-20
7	☐ 15:21-31	☐ 15:32-39	☐ 16:1-12	☐ 16:13-20	☐ 16:21-28	☐ 17:1-13	☐ 17:14-27
8	☐ 18:1-14	☐ 18:15-22	☐ 18:23-35	☐ 19:1-15	☐ 19:16-30	☐ 20:1-16	☐ 20:17-34
9	☐ 21:1-11	☐ 21:12-22	☐ 21:23-32	☐ 21:33-46	☐ 22:1-22	☐ 22:23-33	☐ 22:34-46
10	☐ 23:1-12	☐ 23:13-39	☐ 24:1-14	☐ 24:15-31	☐ 24:32-51	☐ 25:1-13	☐ 25:14-30
11	☐ 25:31-46	☐ 26:1-16	☐ 26:17-35	☐ 26:36-46	☐ 26:47-64	☐ 26:65-75	☐ 27:1-26
12	☐ 27:27-44	☐ 27:45-56	☐ 27:57—28:15	☐ 28:16-20	☐ Mark 1:1	☐ 1:2-6	☐ 1:7-13
13	☐ 1:14-28	☐ 1:29-45	☐ 2:1-12	☐ 2:13-28	☐ 3:1-19	☐ 3:20-35	☐ 4:1-25
14	☐ 4:26-41	☐ 5:1-20	☐ 5:21-43	☐ 6:1-29	☐ 6:30-56	☐ 7:1-23	☐ 7:24-37
15	☐ 8:1-26	☐ 8:27—9:1	☐ 9:2-29	☐ 9:30-50	☐ 10:1-16	☐ 10:17-34	☐ 10:35-52
16	☐ 11:1-16	☐ 11:17-33	☐ 12:1-27	☐ 12:28-44	☐ 13:1-13	☐ 13:14-37	☐ 14:1-26
17	☐ 14:27-52	☐ 14:53-72	☐ 15:1-15	☐ 15:16-47	☐ 16:1-8	☐ 16:9-20	☐ Luke 1:1-4
18	☐ 1:5-25	☐ 1:26-46	☐ 1:47-56	☐ 1:57-80	☐ 2:1-8	☐ 2:9-20	☐ 2:21-39
19	☐ 2:40-52	☐ 3:1-20	☐ 3:21-38	☐ 4:1-13	☐ 4:14-30	☐ 4:31-44	☐ 5:1-26
20	☐ 5:27—6:16	☐ 6:17-38	☐ 6:39-49	☐ 7:1-17	☐ 7:18-23	☐ 7:24-35	☐ 7:36-50
21	☐ 8:1-15	☐ 8:16-25	☐ 8:26-39	☐ 8:40-56	☐ 9:1-17	☐ 9:18-26	☐ 9:27-36
22	☐ 9:37-50	☐ 9:51-62	☐ 10:1-11	☐ 10:12-24	☐ 10:25-37	☐ 10:38-42	☐ 11:1-13
23	☐ 11:14-26	☐ 11:27-36	☐ 11:37-54	☐ 12:1-12	☐ 12:13-21	☐ 12:22-34	☐ 12:35-48
24	☐ 12:49-59	☐ 13:1-9	☐ 13:10-17	☐ 13:18-30	☐ 13:31—14:6	☐ 14:7-14	☐ 14:15-24
25	☐ 14:25-35	☐ 15:1-10	☐ 15:11-21	☐ 15:22-32	☐ 16:1-13	☐ 16:14-22	☐ 16:23-31
26	☐ 17:1-19	☐ 17:20-37	☐ 18:1-14	☐ 18:15-30	☐ 18:31-43	☐ 19:1-10	☐ 19:11-27

Reading Schedule for the Recovery Version of the New Testament with Footnotes

Wk.	Lord's Day	Monday	Tuesday	Wednesday	Thursday	Friday	Saturday
27	Luke 19:28-48	20:1-19	20:20-38	20:39—21:4	21:5-27	21:28-38	22:1-20
28	22:21-38	22:39-54	22:55-71	23:1-43	23:44-56	24:1-12	24:13-35
29	24:36-53	John 1:1-13	1:14-18	1:19-34	1:35-51	2:1-11	2:12-22
30	2:23—3:13	3:14-21	3:22-36	4:1-14	4:15-26	4:27-42	4:43-54
31	5:1-16	5:17-30	5:31-47	6:1-15	6:16-31	6:32-51	6:52-71
32	7:1-9	7:10-24	7:25-36	7:37-52	7:53—8:11	8:12-27	8:28-44
33	8:45-59	9:1-13	9:14-34	9:35—10:9	10:10-30	10:31—11:4	11:5-22
34	11:23-40	11:41-57	12:1-11	12:12-24	12:25-36	12:37-50	13:1-11
35	13:12-30	13:31-38	14:1-6	14:7-20	14:21-31	15:1-11	15:12-27
36	16:1-15	16:16-33	17:1-5	17:6-13	17:14-24	17:25—18:11	18:12-27
37	18:28-40	19:1-16	19:17-30	19:31-42	20:1-13	20:14-18	20:19-22
38	20:23-31	21:1-14	21:15-22	21:23-25	Acts 1:1-8	1:9-14	1:15-26
39	2:1-13	2:14-21	2:22-36	2:37-41	2:42-47	3:1-18	3:19—4:22
40	4:23-37	5:1-16	5:17-32	5:33-42	6:1—7:1	7:2-29	7:30-60
41	8:1-13	8:14-25	8:26-40	9:1-19	9:20-43	10:1-16	10:17-33
42	10:34-48	11:1-18	11:19-30	12:1-25	13:1-12	13:13-43	13:44—14:5
43	14:6-28	15:1-12	15:13-34	15:35—16:5	16:6-18	16:19-40	17:1-18
44	17:19-34	18:1-17	18:18-28	19:1-20	19:21-41	20:1-12	20:13-38
45	21:1-14	21:15-26	21:27-40	22:1-21	22:22-29	22:30—23:11	23:12-15
46	23:16-30	23:31—24:21	24:22—25:5	25:6-27	26:1-13	26:14-32	27:1-26
47	27:27—28:10	28:11-22	28:23-31	Rom 1:1-2	1:3-7	1:8-17	1:18-25
48	1:26—2:10	2:11-29	3:1-20	3:21-31	4:1-12	4:13-25	5:1-11
49	5:12-17	5:18—6:5	6:6-11	6:12-23	7:1-12	7:13-25	8:1-2
50	8:3-6	8:7-13	8:14-25	8:26-39	9:1-18	9:19—10:3	10:4-15
51	10:16—11:10	11:11-22	11:23-36	12:1-3	12:4-21	13:1-14	14:1-12
52	14:13-23	15:1-13	15:14-33	16:1-5	16:6-24	16:25-27	1 Cor 1:1-4

Reading Schedule for the Recovery Version of the New Testament with Footnotes

Wk.	Lord's Day	Monday	Tuesday	Wednesday	Thursday	Friday	Saturday
53	☐ 1 Cor 1:5-9	☐ 1:10-17	☐ 1:18-31	☐ 2:1-5	☐ 2:6-10	☐ 2:11-16	☐ 3:1-9
54	☐ 3:10-13	☐ 3:14-23	☐ 4:1-9	☐ 4:10-21	☐ 5:1-13	☐ 6:1-11	☐ 6:12-20
55	☐ 7:1-16	☐ 7:17-24	☐ 7:25-40	☐ 8:1-13	☐ 9:1-15	☐ 9:16-27	☐ 10:1-4
56	☐ 10:5-13	☐ 10:14-33	☐ 11:1-6	☐ 11:7-16	☐ 11:17-26	☐ 11:27-34	☐ 12:1-11
57	☐ 12:12-22	☐ 12:23-31	☐ 13:1-13	☐ 14:1-12	☐ 14:13-25	☐ 14:26-33	☐ 14:34-40
58	☐ 15:1-19	☐ 15:20-28	☐ 15:29-34	☐ 15:35-49	☐ 15:50-58	☐ 16:1-9	☐ 16:10-24
59	☐ 2 Cor 1:1-4	☐ 1:5-14	☐ 1:15-22	☐ 1:23—2:11	☐ 2:12-17	☐ 3:1-6	☐ 3:7-11
60	☐ 3:12-18	☐ 4:1-6	☐ 4:7-12	☐ 4:13-18	☐ 5:1-8	☐ 5:9-15	☐ 5:16-21
61	☐ 6:1-13	☐ 6:14—7:4	☐ 7:5-16	☐ 8:1-15	☐ 8:16-24	☐ 9:1-15	☐ 10:1-6
62	☐ 10:7-18	☐ 11:1-15	☐ 11:16-33	☐ 12:1-10	☐ 12:11-21	☐ 13:1-10	☐ 13:11-14
63	☐ Gal 1:1-5	☐ 1:6-14	☐ 1:15-24	☐ 2:1-13	☐ 2:14-21	☐ 3:1-4	☐ 3:5-14
64	☐ 3:15-22	☐ 3:23-29	☐ 4:1-7	☐ 4:8-20	☐ 4:21-31	☐ 5:1-12	☐ 5:13-21
65	☐ 5:22-26	☐ 6:1-10	☐ 6:11-15	☐ 6:16-18	☐ Eph 1:1-3	☐ 1:4-6	☐ 1:7-10
66	☐ 1:11-14	☐ 1:15-18	☐ 1:19-23	☐ 2:1-5	☐ 2:6-10	☐ 2:11-14	☐ 2:15-18
67	☐ 2:19-22	☐ 3:1-7	☐ 3:8-13	☐ 3:14-18	☐ 3:19-21	☐ 4:1-4	☐ 4:5-10
68	☐ 4:11-16	☐ 4:17-24	☐ 4:25-32	☐ 5:1-10	☐ 5:11-21	☐ 5:22-26	☐ 5:27-33
69	☐ 6:1-9	☐ 6:10-14	☐ 6:15-18	☐ 6:19-24	☐ Phil 1:1-7	☐ 1:8-18	☐ 1:19-26
70	☐ 1:27—2:4	☐ 2:5-11	☐ 2:12-16	☐ 2:17-30	☐ 3:1-6	☐ 3:7-11	☐ 3:12-16
71	☐ 3:17-21	☐ 4:1-9	☐ 4:10-23	☐ Col 1:1-8	☐ 1:9-13	☐ 1:14-23	☐ 1:24-29
72	☐ 2:1-7	☐ 2:8-15	☐ 2:16-23	☐ 3:1-4	☐ 3:5-15	☐ 3:16-25	☐ 4:1-18
73	☐ 1 Thes 1:1-3	☐ 1:4-10	☐ 2:1-12	☐ 2:13—3:5	☐ 3:6-13	☐ 4:1-10	☐ 4:11—5:11
74	☐ 5:12-28	☐ 2 Thes 1:1-12	☐ 2:1-17	☐ 3:1-18	☐ 1 Tim 1:1-2	☐ 1:3-4	☐ 1:5-14
75	☐ 1:15-20	☐ 2:1-7	☐ 2:8-15	☐ 3:1-13	☐ 3:14—4:5	☐ 4:6-16	☐ 5:1-25
76	☐ 6:1-10	☐ 6:11-21	☐ 2 Tim 1:1-10	☐ 1:11-18	☐ 2:1-15	☐ 2:16-26	☐ 3:1-13
77	☐ 3:14—4:8	☐ 4:9-22	☐ Titus 1:1-4	☐ 1:5-16	☐ 2:1-15	☐ 3:1-8	☐ 3:9-15
78	☐ Philem 1:1-11	☐ 1:12-25	☐ Heb 1:1-2	☐ 1:3-5	☐ 1:6-14	☐ 2:1-9	☐ 2:10-18

Reading Schedule for the Recovery Version of the New Testament with Footnotes

Wk.	Lord's Day	Monday	Tuesday	Wednesday	Thursday	Friday	Saturday
79	☐ Heb 3:1-6	☐ 3:7-19	☐ 4:1-9	☐ 4:10-13	☐ 4:14-16	☐ 5:1-10	☐ 5:11—6:3
80	☐ 6:4-8	☐ 6:9-20	☐ 7:1-10	☐ 7:11-28	☐ 8:1-6	☐ 8:7-13	☐ 9:1-4
81	☐ 9:5-14	☐ 9:15-28	☐ 10:1-18	☐ 10:19-28	☐ 10:29-39	☐ 11:1-6	☐ 11:7-19
82	☐ 11:20-31	☐ 11:32-40	☐ 12:1-2	☐ 12:3-13	☐ 12:14-17	☐ 12:18-26	☐ 12:27-29
83	☐ 13:1-7	☐ 13:8-12	☐ 13:13-15	☐ 13:16-25	☐ James 1:1-8	☐ 1:9-18	☐ 1:19-27
84	☐ 2:1-13	☐ 2:14-26	☐ 3:1-18	☐ 4:1-10	☐ 4:11-17	☐ 5:1-12	☐ 5:13-20
85	☐ 1 Pet 1:1-2	☐ 1:3-4	☐ 1:5	☐ 1:6-9	☐ 1:10-12	☐ 1:13-17	☐ 1:18-25
86	☐ 2:1-3	☐ 2:4-8	☐ 2:9-17	☐ 2:18-25	☐ 3:1-13	☐ 3:14-22	☐ 4:1-6
87	☐ 4:7-16	☐ 4:17-19	☐ 5:1-4	☐ 5:5-9	☐ 5:10-14	☐ 2 Pet 1:1-2	☐ 1:3-4
88	☐ 1:5-8	☐ 1:9-11	☐ 1:12-18	☐ 1:19-21	☐ 2:1-3	☐ 2:4-11	☐ 2:12-22
89	☐ 3:1-6	☐ 3:7-9	☐ 3:10-12	☐ 3:13-15	☐ 3:16	☐ 3:17-18	☐ 1 John 1:1-2
90	☐ 1:3-4	☐ 1:5	☐ 1:6	☐ 1:7	☐ 1:8-10	☐ 2:1-2	☐ 2:3-11
91	☐ 2:12-14	☐ 2:15-19	☐ 2:20-23	☐ 2:24-27	☐ 2:28-29	☐ 3:1-5	☐ 3:6-10
92	☐ 3:11-18	☐ 3:19-24	☐ 4:1-6	☐ 4:7-11	☐ 4:12-15	☐ 4:16—5:3	☐ 5:4-13
93	☐ 5:14-17	☐ 5:18-21	☐ 2 John 1:1-3	☐ 1:4-9	☐ 1:10-13	☐ 3 John 1:1-6	☐ 1:7-14
94	☐ Jude 1:1-4	☐ 1:5-10	☐ 1:11-19	☐ 1:20-25	☐ Rev 1:1-3	☐ 1:4-6	☐ 1:7-11
95	☐ 1:12-13	☐ 1:14-16	☐ 1:17-20	☐ 2:1-6	☐ 2:7	☐ 2:8-9	☐ 2:10-11
96	☐ 2:12-14	☐ 2:15-17	☐ 2:18-23	☐ 2:24-29	☐ 3:1-3	☐ 3:4-6	☐ 3:7-9
97	☐ 3:10-13	☐ 3:14-18	☐ 3:19-22	☐ 4:1-5	☐ 4:6-7	☐ 4:8-11	☐ 5:1-6
98	☐ 5:7-14	☐ 6:1-8	☐ 6:9-17	☐ 7:1-8	☐ 7:9-17	☐ 8:1-6	☐ 8:7-12
99	☐ 8:13—9:11	☐ 9:12-21	☐ 10:1-4	☐ 10:5-11	☐ 11:1-4	☐ 11:5-14	☐ 11:15-19
100	☐ 12:1-4	☐ 12:5-9	☐ 12:10-18	☐ 13:1-10	☐ 13:11-18	☐ 14:1-5	☐ 14:6-12
101	☐ 14:13-20	☐ 15:1-8	☐ 16:1-12	☐ 16:13-21	☐ 17:1-6	☐ 17:7-18	☐ 18:1-8
102	☐ 18:9—19:4	☐ 19:5-10	☐ 19:11-16	☐ 19:17-21	☐ 20:1-6	☐ 20:7-10	☐ 20:11-15
103	☐ 21:1	☐ 21:2	☐ 21:3-8	☐ 21:9-13	☐ 21:14-18	☐ 21:19-21	☐ 21:22-27
104	☐ 22:1	☐ 22:2	☐ 22:3-11	☐ 22:12-15	☐ 22:16-17	☐ 22:18-21	☐

Exo. 30:23-24 You also take the finest spices: of flowing myrrh five hundred *shekels*, and of fragrant cinnamon half as much, two hundred fifty *shekels*, and of fragrant calamus two hundred fifty *shekels*, and of cassia five hundred *shekels*....

1 Tim. 2:5 For there is one God and one Mediator of God and men, the man Christ Jesus.

1 Cor. 6:17 But he who is joined to the Lord is one spirit.

_____
Date

Gen. 6:15-16 And this is how you shall make it: The length of the ark shall be three hundred cubits, its width fifty cubits, and its height thirty cubits....You shall make it with lower, second, and third *stories*.

1 John 2:22 Who is the liar if not he who denies that Jesus is the Christ? This is the antichrist, the one who denies the Father and the Son.

_____
Date

Exo. 30:32-33 Upon the flesh of man it shall not be poured, nor shall you make *any* like it, according to its composition; it is holy; it shall be holy to you. Whoever compounds *any* like it or whoever puts any of it upon a stranger, he shall be cut off from his people.

26 And with it you shall anoint the Tent of Meeting and the Ark of the Testimony.

30 And you shall anoint Aaron and his sons and sanctify them that they may serve Me as priests.

_____
Date

---

1 John 2:20 And you have an anointing from the Holy One, and all of you know.

27 And as for you, the anointing which you have received from Him abides in you, and you have no need that anyone teach you; but as His anointing teaches you concerning all things and is true and is not a lie, and even as it has taught you, abide in Him.

_____
Date

Exo. 30:23-25 You also take the finest spices: of flowing myrrh five hundred *shekels*, and of fragrant cinnamon half as much, two hundred fifty *shekels*, and of fragrant calamus two hundred fifty *shekels*, and of cassia five hundred *shekels*, according to the shekel of the sanctuary, and a hin of olive oil. And you shall make it a holy anointing oil, a fragrant ointment compounded according to the work of a compounder; it shall be a holy anointing oil.

_____
Date

Matt. 28:19 Go therefore and disciple all the nations, baptizing them into the name of the Father and of the Son and of the Holy Spirit.

_____
Date

Week 8 — Day 6   **Today's verses**

John 15:7   If you abide in Me and My words abide in you, ask whatever you will, and it shall be done for you.

_____
Date

Week 8 — Day 5   **Today's verses**

John 14:21, 23   He who has My commandments and keeps them, he is the one who loves Me; and he who loves Me will be loved by My Father, and I will love him and will manifest Myself to him....If anyone loves Me, he will keep My word, and My Father will love him, and We will come to him and make an abode with him.

1 John 2:27   And as for you, the anointing which you have received from Him abides in you, and you have no need that anyone teach you; but as His anointing teaches you concerning all things and is true and is not a lie, and even as it has taught you, abide in Him.

_____
Date

Week 8 — Day 4   **Today's verses**

Rev. 21:3   And I heard a loud voice out of the throne, saying, Behold, the tabernacle of God is with men...

22   And I saw no temple in it, for the Lord God the Almighty and the Lamb are its temple.

2:17   ...To him who overcomes, to him I will give of the hidden manna...

_____
Date

Week 8 — Day 3   **Today's verses**

Psa. 90:1   O Lord, You have been our dwelling place / In all generations.

91:1   He who dwells in the secret place of the Most High / Will abide in the shadow of the Almighty.

9   For You have made Jehovah, _who is_ my refuge, / Even the Most High, Your habitation.

_____
Date

Week 8 — Day 2   **Today's verses**

1 John 2:24   As for you, that which you heard from the beginning, let it abide in you. If that which you heard from the beginning abides in you, you also will abide in the Son and in the Father.

John 14:17   _Even_ the Spirit of reality, whom the world cannot receive, because it does not behold Him or know _Him; but_ you know Him, because He abides with you and shall be in you.

_____
Date

Week 8 — Day 1   **Today's verses**

1 John 3:22-24   ...Whatever we ask we receive from Him because we keep His commandments and do the things that are pleasing in His sight. And this is His commandment, that we believe in the name of His Son Jesus Christ and love one another, even as He gave a commandment to us. And he who keeps His commandments abides in Him, and He in him. And in this we know that He abides in us, by the Spirit whom He gave to us.

_____
Date

Week 9 — Day 4 · Today's verses

1 John 3:3-4 And everyone who has this hope set on Him purifies himself, even as He is pure. Everyone who practices sin practices lawlessness also, and sin is lawlessness.

6 Everyone who abides in Him does not sin; everyone who sins has not seen Him or known Him.

9 Everyone who has been begotten of God does not practice sin, because His seed abides in him; and he cannot sin, because he has been begotten of God.

Date

Week 9 — Day 5 · Today's verses

Phil. 3:9 And be found in Him, not having my own righteousness which is out of the law, but that which is through faith in Christ, the righteousness which is out of God *and* based on faith.

2 Cor. 5:21 Him who did not know sin He made sin on our behalf that we might become the righteousness of God in Him.

2 Pet. 3:13 But according to His promise we are expecting new heavens and a new earth, in which righteousness dwells.

Date

Week 9 — Day 6 · Today's verses

Rom. 14:17 For the kingdom of God is not eating and drinking, but righteousness and peace and joy in the Holy Spirit.

Psa. 89:14 Righteousness and justice are the foundation of Your throne; / Lovingkindness and truth go before Your face.

Heb. 1:8-9 But of the Son, "Your throne, O God, is forever and ever, and the scepter of uprightness is the scepter of Your kingdom. You have loved righteousness and hated lawlessness; therefore God, Your God, has anointed You with the oil of exultant joy above Your partners."

Date

Week 9 — Day 1 · Today's verses

Rom. 1:17 ...As it is written, "But the righteous shall have life and live by faith."

Rev. 16:7 ...Yes, Lord God the Almighty, true and righteous are Your judgments.

1 John 1:9 If we confess our sins, He is faithful and righteous to forgive us our sins and cleanse us from all unrighteousness.

2:1 ...If anyone sins, we have an Advocate with the Father, Jesus Christ the Righteous.

Date

Week 9 — Day 2 · Today's verses

Matt. 5:20 ...Unless your righteousness surpasses that of the scribes and Pharisees, you shall by no means enter into the kingdom of the heavens.

1 Cor. 1:30 But of Him you are in Christ Jesus, who became wisdom to us from God: both righteousness and sanctification and redemption.

Acts 13:39 And from all the things from which you were not able to be justified by the law of Moses, in this One everyone who believes is justified.

Rev. 19:8 And it was given to her that she should be clothed in fine linen, bright *and* clean; for the fine linen is the righteousnesses of the saints.

Date

Week 9 — Day 3 · Today's verses

1 John 2:29 If you know that He is righteous, you know that everyone who practices righteousness also has been begotten of Him.

3:7 Little children, let no one lead you astray; he who practices righteousness is righteous, even as He is righteous.

Rev. 15:3 And they sing the song of Moses, the slave of God, and the song of the Lamb, saying, Great and wonderful are Your works, Lord God the Almighty! Righteous and true are Your ways, O King of the nations!

Eph. 4:24 And put on the new man, which was created according to God in righteousness and holiness of the reality.

Date

Week 10 — Day 4   Today's verses

1 John But whoever keeps His word, truly in this
2:5 one the love of God has been perfected. In this we know that we are in Him.

7-8 Beloved, I am not writing a new commandment to you but an old commandment, which you have had from the beginning; the old commandment is the word which you heard. Yet again a new commandment I am writing to you, which is true in Him and in you because the darkness is passing away and the true light is already shining.

3:23 And this is His commandment, that we believe in the name of His Son Jesus Christ and love one another, even as He gave a commandment to us.

Date

Week 10 — Day 5   Today's verses

2 John And now I ask you, lady, not as writing a
5-6 new commandment to you but that which we have had from the beginning, that we love one another. And this is love, that we walk according to His commandments. This is the commandment, even as you heard from the beginning, that you walk in love.

Date

Week 10 — Day 6   Today's verses

1 John And we know and have believed the love
4:16-18 which God has in us. God is love, and he who abides in love abides in God and God abides in him. In this has love been perfected with us, that we may have boldness in the day of the judgment because even as He is, so also are we in this world. There is no fear in love, but perfect love casts out fear because fear has punishment, and he who fears has not been perfected in love.

Date

Week 10 — Day 1   Today's verses

1 John Beloved, let us love one another, because
4:7-10 love is of God, and everyone who loves has been begotten of God and knows God. He who does not love has not known God, because God is love. In this the love of God was manifested among us, that God sent His only begotten Son into the world that we might have life and live through Him. Herein is love, not that we have loved God but that He loved us and sent His Son as a propitiation for our sins.

Rom. ...The love of God has been poured out in
5:5 our hearts through the Holy Spirit, who has been given to us.

Date

Week 10 — Day 2   Today's verses

Rom. Who shall separate us from the love of
8:35-39 Christ? Shall tribulation or anguish or persecution or famine or nakedness or peril or sword? As it is written, "For Your sake we are being put to death all day long; we have been accounted as sheep for slaughter." But in all these things we more than conquer through Him who loved us. For I am persuaded that neither death nor life nor angels nor principalities nor things present nor things to come nor powers nor height nor depth nor any other creature will be able to separate us from the love of God, which is in Christ Jesus our Lord.

Date

Week 10 — Day 3   Today's verses

1 John We know that we have passed out of
3:14 death into life because we love the brothers. He who does not love abides in death.

5:1 Everyone who believes that Jesus is the Christ has been begotten of God, and everyone who loves Him who has begotten loves him also who has been begotten of Him.

Date

Week 11 — Day 1   Today's verses

1 John   This is He who came through water and
5:6-9   blood, Jesus Christ; not in the water only,
but in the water and in the blood; and
the Spirit is He who testifies, because the
Spirit is the reality. For there are three who
testify, the Spirit and the water and the
blood, and the three are unto the one
thing. If we receive the testimony of men,
the testimony of God is greater, because
this is the testimony of God that He has
testified concerning His Son.

Date

Week 11 — Day 2   Today's verses

Matt.   And having been baptized, Jesus went up
3:16-17   immediately from the water, and behold, the
heavens were opened to Him, and He saw
the Spirit of God descending like a dove and
coming upon Him. And behold, a voice out
of the heavens, saying, This is My Son, the
Beloved, in whom I have found My delight.

27:54   Now the centurion and those with him
guarding Jesus, when they saw...the things
that happened, became greatly frightened,
saying, Truly this was the Son of God.

John   But when the Comforter comes, whom I will
15:26   send to you from the Father, the Spirit of reality, who proceeds from the Father, He will
testify concerning Me.

Date

Week 11 — Day 3   Today's verses

1 John   He who believes into the Son of God has
5:10-13   the testimony in himself; he who does not
believe God has made Him a liar because
he has not believed in the testimony
which God has testified concerning His
Son. And this is the testimony, that God
gave to us eternal life and this life is in His
Son. He who has the Son has the life; he
who does not have the Son of God does
not have the life. I have written these
things to you that you may know that you
have eternal life, to you who believe into
the name of the Son of God.

Date

Week 11 — Day 4   Today's verses

1 John   If anyone sees his brother sinning a sin not
5:16-17   unto death, he shall ask and he will give
life to him, to those sinning not unto
death. There is a sin unto death; I do not
say that he should make request concerning that. All unrighteousness is sin, and
there is sin not unto death.

Rom.   So we who are many are one Body in
12:5   Christ, and individually members one of
another.

Date

Week 11 — Day 5   Today's verses

1 John   And this is the boldness which we have
5:14-15   toward Him, that if we ask anything
according to His will, He hears us. And if
we know that He hears us in whatever we
ask, we know that we have the requests
which we have asked from Him.

John   If you abide in Me and My words abide in
15:7   you, ask whatever you will, and it shall be
done for you.

Date

Week 11 — Day 6   Today's verses

John   And in that day you will ask Me nothing.
16:23-24   Truly, truly, I say to you, Whatever you ask
the Father in My name, He will give to
you. Until now you have asked for nothing in My name; ask and you shall
receive, that your joy may be made full.

Amos   Surely the Lord Jehovah will not do any-
3:7   thing unless He reveals His secret to His
servants the prophets.

Date

Week 12 — Day 4   Today's verses

1 John 5:4-5   For everything that has been begotten of God overcomes the world; and this is the victory which has overcome the world—our faith. And who is he who overcomes the world except him who believes that Jesus is the Son of God?

18   We know that everyone who is begotten of God does not sin, but he who has been begotten of God keeps himself, and the evil one does not touch him.

Date

Week 12 — Day 5   Today's verses

1 John 2:18   Young children, it is the last hour; and even as you heard that antichrist is coming, even now many antichrists have come; whereby we know that it is the last hour.

22   Who is the liar if not he who denies that Jesus is the Christ? This is the antichrist, the one who denies the Father and the Son.

5:21   Little children, guard yourselves from idols.

Date

Week 12 — Day 6   Today's verses

3 John 9-10   I wrote something to the church; but Diotrephes, who loves to be first among them, does not receive us. For this reason, if I come, I will bring to remembrance his works which he does, babbling against us with evil words; and not being satisfied with these, neither does he himself receive the brothers, and those intending to *do* so he forbids and casts out of the church.

2 John 7   For many deceivers went out into the world, those who do not confess Jesus Christ coming in the flesh. This is the deceiver and the antichrist.

Date

Week 12 — Day 1   Today's verses

John 17:2-3   Even as You have given Him authority over all flesh to give eternal life to all whom You have given Him. And this is eternal life, that they may know You, the only true God, and Him whom You have sent, Jesus Christ.

1 John 5:20   And we know that the Son of God has come and has given us an understanding that we might know Him who is true; and we are in Him who is true, in His Son Jesus Christ. This is the true God and eternal life.

Date

Week 12 — Day 2   Today's verses

Col. 2:9   For in Him dwells all the fullness of the Godhead bodily.

Eph. 1:17   That the God of our Lord Jesus Christ, the Father of glory, may give to you a spirit of wisdom and revelation in the full knowledge of Him.

1 John 5:11   And this is the testimony, that God gave to us eternal life and this life is in His Son.

Date

Week 12 — Day 3   Today's verses

1 John 2:12-14   I write to you, little children, because your sins have been forgiven you because of His name. I write to you, fathers, because you know Him who is from the beginning. I write to you, young men, because you have overcome the evil one. I write to you, young children, because you know the Father. I have written to you, fathers, because you know Him who is from the beginning. I have written to you, young men, because you are strong, and the word of God abides in you and you have overcome the evil one.

4:4   You are of God, little children; and you have overcome them because greater is He who is in you than he who is in the world.

Date